Color-Blend
Appliqué

COLOR-BLEND APPLIQUÉ

JANE TOWNSWICK

Martingale™
& COMPANY

CREDITS

President • *Nancy J. Martin*
CEO • *Daniel J. Martin*
Publisher • *Jane Hamada*
Editorial Director • *Mary V. Green*
Managing Editor • *Tina Cook*
Technical Editor • *Ursula Reikes*
Copy Editor • *Allison A. Merrill*
Design Director • *Stan Green*
Illustrator • *Laurel Strand*
Cover and Text Designer • *Trina Stahl*
Photographer • *Brent Kane*

That Patchwork Place® is an imprint of
Martingale & Company™.

Color-Blend Appliqué
© 2003 by Jane Townswick

Martingale & Company
20205 144th Avenue NE
Woodinville, WA 98072-8478 USA
www.martingale-pub.com

Printed in China
08 07 06 05 04 03   8 7 6 5 4 3 2

MISSION STATEMENT

*We are dedicated to providing quality products
and service by working together to inspire creativity and
to enrich the lives we touch.*

Library of Congress Cataloging-in-Publication Data

Townswick, Jane.
  Color-blend appliqué / Jane Townswick.
     p.   cm.
  ISBN 1-56477-450-3
  1. Appliqué—Patterns.   2. Quilting—Patterns.   3. Color in art.   I. Title.
  TT779 .T693 2003
  746.44'5—dc21
                                                  2002011801

DEDICATION

To MY MOTHER, Genevieve Elizabeth Townswick, the kindest, gentlest person I have ever known. Thank you for teaching me to live life with courage and to trust God in everything.

ACKNOWLEDGMENTS

I GIVE THANKS to my brother, Gary Townswick, who is a much better artist than I will ever be, for sharing his artistic expertise and innovative ideas on color with me.

My ability to come up with new designs and innovative techniques for hand appliqué comes in large part from the creative atmosphere at Gail Kessler's shop, Ladyfingers Sewing Studio, in Oley, Pennsylvania. Gail has given me the opportunity to teach appliqué classes there since 1997, and her encouragement and inspiration have made me grow more as an artist and teacher than I ever dreamed possible. For these things, and for her friendship, I am grateful.

I am indebted to Mary Green for believing in me as a writer and as an appliqué artist, and to Ursula Reikes, my editor, for bringing clarity and polish to my words. My thanks also go to everyone at Martingale & Company who lent their talent and creativity to producing this book.

CONTENTS

INTRODUCTION

I LOOK AT the world around me and see appliqué everywhere. Last year, I noticed a photograph of a beautiful pink flower on a wall of a shop where I like to ship packages. The flower had delicate, dark red veins spreading through each petal. The photo stayed in my mind, and I began to wonder how I could create a hand-appliqué design of the flower. The result is my color-blended hibiscus below right. Rather than inking dark veins on a single fabric, I used many different fabrics in similar values to create a flower that looks as if it is bathed in sunlight and shadow.

Photo courtesy of Jeanette Schlegel.

My color-blending concept involves combining many fabrics within a single appliqué shape to create rich visual depth in your work. It is an easy process that produces artistic effects, allowing you to become a "painter in fabric." Color blending will help you express your unique color sensibilities in ways you may never have been able to before.

Each of the twelve blocks in this book features a list of techniques used in creating that block. In addition to color blending, you will find my new steep-point technique, tricks for doing complex unit and free-form appliqué, tips for making bias stems and vines using a Hera marker, techniques for sandwiching narrow strips of color between appliqué shapes, methods for incorporating sheer metallic fabric, and a variety of ways to ink details onto fabric. The blocks are presented in a progression from easy to more intricate. Read through "Appliqué Basics" on pages 9–16. Then choose a block that features techniques you wish to learn. Move on to other blocks as you desire.

For great inspiration, spend some time looking through "Gallery of Quilts" on pages 19–35. You'll see the innovative ways my students have used my color-blending and hand-appliqué techniques in their beautiful quilts. I hope you will use this book as a teach-yourself guide to expanding your appliqué skills, and let your own creativity run free in future projects.

Happy stitching!

Jane Townswick

Appliqué Basics

The more you love hand appliqué, the more you will enjoy discovering new techniques and designs you want to stitch. Because appliqué is an ever-changing art form, it continually offers opportunities to develop new skills and refine them in many ways. On the following pages, you will find a list of the tools, supplies, and techniques I like for hand appliqué. Check them out and add the ones you enjoy to your repertoire of favorites.

Tools and Supplies

Using the right equipment makes any quiltmaking task easier, more accurate, and more fun. Many of the products you see on this page are available at your local quilt shops. However, if you have difficulty finding any of the products, consult "Resources" on page 125.

List of Tools and Supplies

- 9½", 12", and 15" square acrylic rulers with ⅛" markings
- 1" x 6", 3" x 18", and 6" x 24" acrylic rulers with ⅛" markings
- Large- and medium-sized rotary cutters
- 24" x 36" self-healing rotary-cutting mat
- Silk pins
- Jeana Kimball's Foxglove Cottage extra-sharp appliqué pins
- Jeana Kimball's Foxglove Cottage size #11 straw needles
- Colonial size #12 Sharp needles
- 100-denier silk thread by YLI, especially colors 217, 226, 235, 239, and 242
- Well-fitting thimble
- Round wooden toothpicks with sharp tips; 4" bamboo skewers also work well
- 3½" Gingher embroidery scissors with micro-serrated blade (for cutting fabric)
- Clover patchwork scissors (for cutting paper)
- Avery water-soluble glue pen (for glue-basting fabric)
- Freezer paper, template plastic, or CAT paper* (for making templates)
- Circle stencils (found in office- and art-supply stores)
- Sharpie permanent marking pen (for marking templates)
- Clover water-soluble white marking pen (for marking fabric)
- Clover Eraser pen (for removing water-soluble pen marks without water)
- Quilter's Choice silver and white pencils (for marking fabric)
- Pigma .01 mm marking pens in black and in colors (for inking fabric)
- Small wooden "finger-creasing" iron

CAT (Clear Appliqué Template) paper is an opaque paper with an adhesive back that adheres easily to fabric. It is available from Ladyfingers Sewing Studio (see page 125).

THE APPLIQUÉ STITCH

Follow these steps to keep your body comfortable while you work and to make your appliqué stitches nearly invisible.

GETTING STARTED

Start by determining the correct thread length for your arm.

Holding the end of 100-denier silk thread between the thumb and index finger of one hand, with the other hand pull the spool gently down to your elbow and cut the thread at that point.

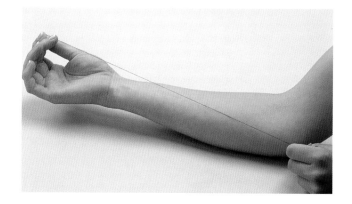

ANCHORING A NEEDLE
AND SILK THREAD

1. To anchor a strand of 100-denier silk thread onto the eye of a needle, start by threading a needle with thread cut to the correct length for you. Make a loop with the short end of the thread and insert the needle into the loop. Make sure that the short end of the thread is on *top* of the long end. Hold the loop to the needle with your index finger.

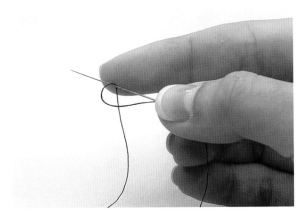

2. Holding the needle with your other hand, gently pull on the long end of the thread, allowing the loop to slide down along the shank of the needle and "lock" onto the eye of the needle.

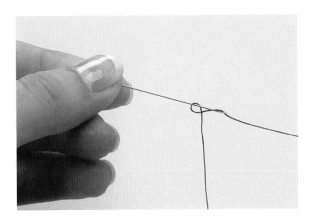

3. Finally, make a small quilter's knot at the long end of the thread. Hold the needle and the long end of the thread together in your right hand. With your left hand, wind the end of the thread gently 5 or 6 times around the needle. Slide the wound portion of thread down the shank of the needle so that it lies between your right thumb and forefinger.

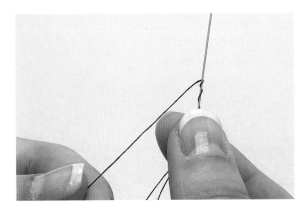

4. With your left hand, gently pull the needle up while still holding the wound threads between your right thumb and forefinger, until the wound portion of thread forms a small knot at the end of the thread.

STARTING TO STITCH

1. Cut a 3/16" seam allowance around an appliqué shape and pin it in place on the background fabric. Bring a threaded needle up just inside the marked turning line on the appliqué shape. Place your left thumb alongside the marked turning line, and support the background and appliqué fabrics with your middle finger underneath.

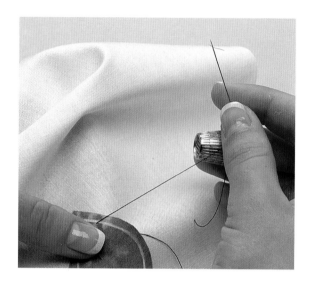

2. Using the tip of a round wooden toothpick or a bamboo skewer, gently tuck the seam allowance under, supporting it with your underneath finger. When you are happy with the way the folded edge looks, pinch the fabric gently between your thumb and underneath finger to make the fold crisp without distorting the fabric.

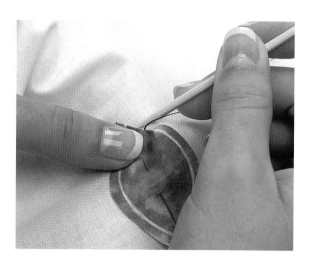

3. Pull the thread out at a 90° angle to the creased fold. Holding your needle vertically, insert it into the background fabric, *just* to the right of the thread and next to the folded edge of the appliqué shape.

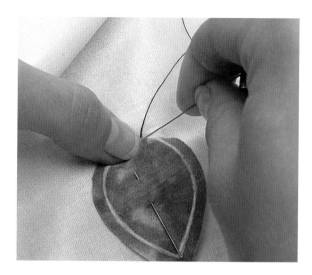

4. Gently lower your hand and allow the needle to come back up through the background fabric and catch the very tip of the fold on the appliqué shape. This easy, natural motion will allow you to establish the perfect stitch length for your hand and arm. It will also help you stitch more comfortably for longer periods of time and avoid angling your wrist repetitively as you sew.

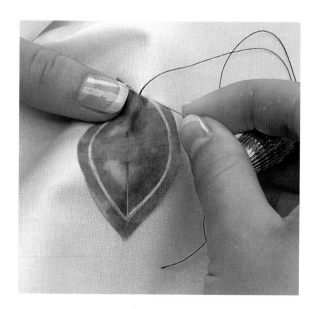

5. Pull the needle and thread out at a 90° angle again. This will show you the exact point at which you should insert the needle for the next stitch: just to the right of the thread and next to the fold. Continue making each appliqué stitch in the same manner.

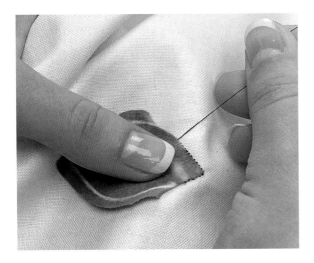

ENDING A THREAD

1. To end a thread, insert the needle into the background fabric as if you were going to take another stitch, but bring it all the way through to the back side of your work. Wind the thread around the needle two or three times. Then insert the tip of the needle between the background fabric and the appliqué shape, as close as possible to the point where the thread emerges from the fabric. Bring the needle up approximately ½" away.

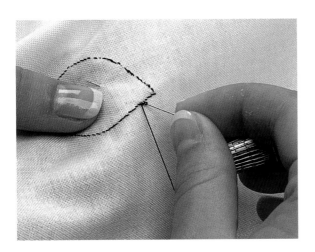

2. Pull the thread all the way out of the background fabric, leaving a small French knot on the surface. Tug on the thread gently to pop the French knot between the background and appliqué fabrics.

3. Clip the thread close to the surface of the fabric.

FINISHING

All of the blocks in this book involve the same finishing techniques. To give your appliqué a crisp finish, spray the back side of your work lightly with water and press it with a dry iron set at the cotton setting. Spray the front side of the block and press again. Place the block on a rotary-cutting mat and center a 9½" square acrylic ruler over it. Use a rotary cutter to trim the finished block to 9½" square.

HERA BIAS STRIPS

Whenever you need to make bias stems (or vines) in any width, use a Hera marker to score easy-to-see, accurate turning lines, and a rotary cutter to cut seam allowances.

1. Place the stem fabric *wrong* side up on a cutting mat. This is important to ensure that the seam allowances on your finished stems will automatically want to turn under toward the wrong side of the fabric. Align the 45°-angle line on a 3" x 18" ruler with a straight edge of the fabric to establish the true bias angle. Make sure that the distance along the ruler's edge is long enough for the stem you want to cut.

2. Using a Hera marker as you would a rotary cutter, slowly move the marker back and forth along the edge of the ruler slowly. As you do this, keep the marker perpendicular to the fabric and put a lot of pressure on it.

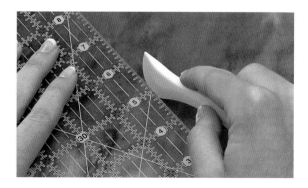

3. Move the ruler aside and check to make sure that the first turning line you scored is easily visible and perfectly straight.

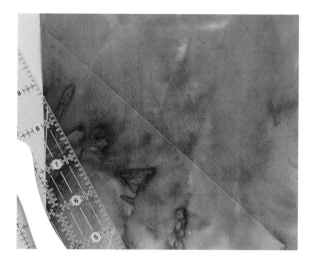

4. Determine the desired finished width of your bias stem and align that mark on the ruler with the first scored turning line. Using the Hera marker again, score a second turning line. The more carefully and accurately you do this step, the happier you will be with your finished stem. The stem in the photo below will be ⅛" wide when finished.

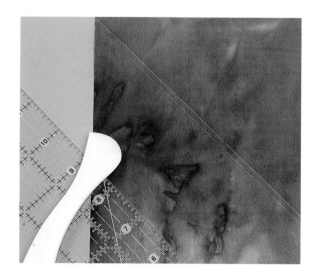

5. To add a seam allowance to each side of the stem, align the ⅛" mark on the ruler with *each* of the scored turning lines and cut along the ruler with a rotary cutter. Rotary cut the ends of the stem perpendicular to the turning lines.

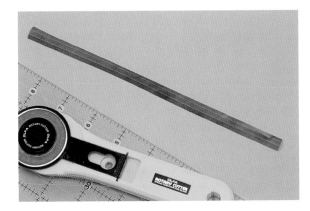

STEEP POINTS

Several designs in this book feature my steep-point technique. No matter how many fabrics are included in it, you can use this technique to stitch any steep point with ease.

1. Cut a ¼" seam allowance around the left edge of the point shape and a regular ³⁄₁₆" seam allowance around the right edge.

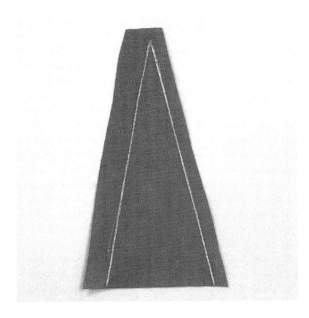

2. Stitch the right edge all the way up to the very tip of the point. Insert the needle into the background at the very tip, and bring the thread all the way through to the back side of your work. Take a lock stitch over your final appliqué stitch. Clip the thread, leaving a 6" tail of thread hanging; you will need this thread to tie a knot after finishing the second side of the point. Clip the seam allowance on the left edge of the point shape ½" from the tip of the point. Turn under and stitch the seam allowance from the clip to the bottom on the left side of the point shape.

3. On the back side of your work, insert the tip of one blade of sharp embroidery scissors into the background fabric. The blade tip should be approximately ¼" below the stitched line at the open area of the point. Cut the background fabric only, straight up to the very tip of the point. Also clip up to (but not through) the stitched line as shown.

4. Gently lift the background fabric and fold it over to create a turning line for the unstitched area of the steep point. Press the fabric with your finger to crease the fold without distorting the fabric. When you are happy with the way the folded edge looks, coat the tip of a toothpick with glue and run the glue underneath the fold. Then pinch the fabric in place with your fingers.

5. Use your left index finger to push the seam allowance of the unstitched point through to the back side of your work.

6. On the front side of your work, you will have a perfectly accurate, glue-basted fold at the unstitched area on the left side of the steep point. Thread a needle with thread that matches your background fabric and stitch this area, ending at the very tip of the steep point.

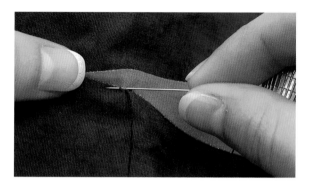

7. After you take the last stitch at the very tip of the steep point, bring the needle all the way through to the back side of your work. Using this thread and the 6" tail of thread left hanging from step 2 on page 15, tie 2 knots and clip the threads close to the knots.

COLOR BLENDING FABRICS

MY NEW COLOR-BLENDING technique involves combining many different fabrics within an appliqué shape. The key to creating this artistic look is to use similar values (the lightness or darkness of a color) in neighboring individual pieces. Here are some examples illustrating this concept and some guidelines to follow as you select fabrics for the designs in this book. After reading through them, gather some fabrics from your stash and start playing with color and value sequences of your own.

◆ Value is more important than color itself for color blending. Use similar values beside each other and they will blend together visually, no matter what colors you choose. You can create a progression from light to dark, or from dark to light.

◆ You can also position lights in the center and move toward darks on either side, or vice versa.

◆ Sudden changes in value will draw the eye to a specific area. Unless you wish to create this particular effect (which can sometimes be a creative option), avoid abrupt changes in value.

◆ You can mix values within an appliqué shape, highlighting certain areas, as in this anthurium blossom. While a basic progression of values occurs throughout the shape, lighter colors draw the eye to certain areas of the flower.

◆ You can use small-scale multicolored prints, tone-on-tone fabrics, solids, hand-painted fabrics, batiks, or any other fabric that pleases you for color blending. As long as you keep values similar between neighboring pieces, you can create exciting visual effects.

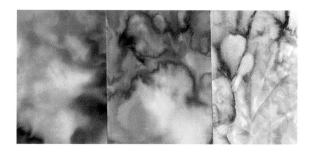

◆ Avoid plaids, stripes, and high-contrast prints for color blending. These fabrics tend to draw attention, which makes them less effective for color blending.

GALLERY OF QUILTS

In this gallery, you'll see an array of gorgeous floral quilts, from pillows and table runners to wall hangings and larger quilts. Each project was made by a quilter who has attended one or more of my workshops at Ladyfingers Sewing Studio in Oley, Pennsylvania. Some of these projects feature one block, while others display a selection of favorite designs or the entire group of twelve blocks. In my workshops, the only rules are that each person must explore new techniques and decide which ones they like. Then they can enjoy using these techniques to stitch appliqué projects. All of the quilts shown on the following pages are examples of what can happen when an inner sense of creativity takes over and leads a quilter into an adventure with hand appliqué.

MY BLUE ANTHURIUM, 42" x 42"

The beauty of Jane's designs is that they look complicated, but her construction techniques are incredibly simple! Both my corner appliqué and trapunto areas were inspired by her Daffodil block. This wall hanging challenged me to use color differently, so "My Blue Anthurium" was an experiment as well as a reminder of the four years I lived in Hawaii. I love needleturn appliqué and hand quilting, and I can hardly wait to tackle future blocks by Jane.
—Monteen Bard, Carlisle, Pennsylvania

HEARTS AND FLOWERS—SATURDAY'S GARDEN, 51" x 64"

Look! It's a riot of summer blossoms spreading across the garden in glorious colors! From the realistic to the fantastic, fabrics provide a joyous reflection of the infinite detail in God's creations.

This quilt recalls happy memories of Saturdays spent in Oley, Pennsylvania, attending Jane's appliqué class at Ladyfingers Sewing Studio. Jane's incredible techniques and beautiful designs are inspirational.

My goal for this quilt was to be brave and use background colors other than white. It's been quite an adventure! Be on the lookout for delicately inked flower veins, single-strand silk French knots and bullions, as well as funky bouclé yarns and more than 200 beads in a single flower center.

—Diana Lynn Channer, Schwenksville, Pennsylvania

19 Times the Square Root of 2, 48" x 48"

The title of my quilt comes from the measurement of the side of the large Log Cabin block, as computed by my husband, Bob. Jane's color-blending technique introduces an entirely new approach to shading and lighting to achieve depth in your work.

—Kathleen DeCarli, Downingtown, Pennsylvania

AME'S GARDEN, 23" x 23"

I came to Jane's appliqué class not knowing how to appliqué and having done nothing but primitive quilts. Jane's color-blending technique gave me the confidence to try new things with color. I even dyed some of my own fabric for this piece! As for being able to appliqué, now I do not like to piece quilts.

—Christine Dreazen, Reading, Pennsylvania

GARDEN ELEGANCE, 52" x 52"

Two years ago I started appliquéing the blocks of this quilt. With Jane's incredible techniques and encouragement from other classmates, my second quilt is complete. My interest in gardening and flowers influenced the choice of colors in this quilt. Embroidery was used to add shadowing to the calla lilies, and French knots form the stamens of the blue poppies.

—Diane Fair, Birdsboro, Pennsylvania

PURPLE MAJESTY, 35" x 35"

When I learned of Jane's appliqué classes at the Ladyfingers Sewing Studio in Oley, Pennsylvania, I lost no time in joining. I knew it would be a great opportunity to perfect my appliqué skills. Jane's special techniques make the most difficult-looking blocks fun and easy to do. Her color-blending technique expanded my use of color and I was surprised at how purple kept appearing in all my blocks. This was my first attempt at hand quilting and I loved it! Jane's classes are so much fun that my aunt and I look forward to our day in Oley on the second Saturday of each month.

—Peggy Heverin, Elkton, Maryland

SATURDAYS IN THE GARDEN, 35"x 35"

I love doing appliqué using Jane's techniques. Working with units gives me freedom to position a design within a block, and I am learning to play with color. In "Saturdays in the Garden," I had fun adapting Jane's designs for the quilting in the setting triangles.

—Karen Carnwath Johnson, Upper Milford, Pennsylvania

SILK FLOWERS, 45" x 58"

Jane's appliqué designs provided excellent inspiration for this quilt. I really love to hand appliqué and hand quilt, but not in squares. Her designs helped me express my ideas in appliqué and quilted silk. I used to paint flowers; now with Jane's technique, I can appliqué them. I started this quilt on December 15, 2001, and finished it on March 20, 2002.
—Rose M. King, Wyomissing, Pennsylvania

HEARTWARMING HIBISCUS, 16" x 16"

Jane turned my first experience with hand appliqué into a passion! Her innovative techniques have given me the freedom to find my own style and experiment with fabric, color, and texture. She always stresses to her students to stitch what pleases us and to think outside the box. My creativity has exploded since taking Jane's course. My mother-in-law and friend, Eveline Kuring, assembled my pillow.

—Debi Kuring, Blandon, Pennsylvania

FLOWERS JANE'S WAY, 16" x 52½"

In the fall of 1997, I signed up for a few classes with a woman by the name of Jane Townswick to improve my appliqué skills. Four and a half years later, I am still going to Oley, Pennsylvania, on the fourth Saturday of the month to stitch with and learn from Jane, whom I now consider a friend as well as a teacher. I go to see what new and exciting designs she has for us to stitch that day. "Flowers Jane's Way" is a small example featuring some of her wonderful blocks and innovative techniques. It was machine quilted by Carol Heisler.
—Dorothy W. Murdoch, West Chester, Pennsylvania

CULTIVATING ENJOYMENT, 55" x 55"

This quilt took two years to "grow." I carefully selected the seeds of my blocks, and then I raised them using Jane's techniques. Finally, when my nine flowers bloomed, I did what all planters do: I asked friends to enjoy my garden with me. I give thanks to Terry P. Clark, whose setting, piecing, and machine quilting (see "Resources," page 125) gave my flower beds their final shape.

—Gayle Lynn Rosenbach, Springfield, New Jersey

SPRING FEVER, 32½" x 32½"

I used batiks for the flowers, background, and watercolor-style Trip around the World border. Jane's techniques make the most complicated-looking blocks very easy. As a novice in the art of appliqué, I'm very pleased with the skill level I've achieved in a few lessons.

—Lucille Gery Schantz, Macungie, Pennsylvania

FLOWER POWER, 42" x 42"

"Flower Power" is hand appliquéd, machine sewn, and machine quilted. It took me two years to get enough nerve to join Jane's appliqué class: I am a "folk-art wing-it" sort of appliquer, and Jane's precise, crisp designs looked too difficult for me. Wrong! Her techniques are so easy that even I am able to execute them. I call my piece "Flower Power" because the flower patterns are so strong and beautiful. The setting for this quilt was inspired by knot-garden designs.

—Nan Tischler, Downingtown, Pennsylvania

THE GARDEN PATCH, 33" x 33"

I was in awe over Jane's portfolio—full of beautiful flowers. I had to try to create them. Thus, the second Saturday of every month, my niece and I traveled for an hour and forty-five minutes to Jane's class at Ladyfingers Sewing Studio in Oley, Pennsylvania. Jane's appliqué techniques made the most complicated block seem easy and her color-blending techniques made my blossoms come alive. "The Garden Patch" is for my daughter, who was ever in my thoughts as I contentedly stitched the hours away.

—Donna Truitt, Elkton, Maryland

SERENDIPITY, 38" x 39"

This quilt grew from the choices I made for the very first block we sewed in our appliqué class with Jane. I wanted natural-looking daffodils on a light background. I took tones, tints, hues, and shades from my background and the vases to build my quilt. Jane teaches much more than how to sew a fine stitch. Thank you, Jane.
—Darlene Tulley, Kenhorst, Pennsylvania

WILLIAMSBURG FOLLOWING, 15" x 15"

Little did I realize when I walked into a shop in Pennsylvania that I would see appliqué taken to the next level. When I first saw Jane's work, I was hooked. Who knew that I would even travel to Williamsburg, Virginia, to take a class with her? Thank you, Jane, for all of the wonderful techniques you have developed!
—Joan Flanigan-Clarke, Mahwah, New Jersey

FLORAL APPLIQUÉ

ALL OF THE blocks in this book measure 9" finished (9½" including seam allowances) and are intended to be set on point. If you wish to set your blocks straight, you will need to make your background squares at least 12" finished.

DAFFODILS
Page 38

ANTHURIUMS
Page 44

ORCHID
Page 65

HIBISCUS
Page 71

BLEEDING HEARTS
Page 94

BIRDS-OF-PARADISE
Page 102

BLOCKS

BEGONIA
Page 50

IRIS
Page 57

CALLA LILY
Page 80

POPPIES
Page 88

TULIPS
Page 108

ROSE
Page 115

DAFFODILS

My students often ask me to create appliqué designs for flowers they love. This Daffodil block took a few months to "percolate" because I wanted to come up with an easy and effective technique for making the center "trumpets" look three-dimensional, without using any templates. Once that idea jelled, the rest of the design fell into place easily.

TECHNIQUES

Hera bias strips (stems)
Needle sculpting (daffodils)
Echoing colors (daffodils, vase)
No-template appliqué (trumpet centers)
Reverse appliqué (rims of trumpet centers)

FABRICS AND SUPPLIES

- 11" square of fabric for background
- 1 fat quarter of fabric for stems
- Eighteen 1½" squares of fabric for leaves
- 15 assorted 2" squares of fabric for lower petals
- 15 assorted 1½" squares of fabric for upper petals
- Three 1½" squares of fabric for rims of trumpet centers
- Three 2" squares of fabric for trumpet centers
- 6" square of fabric for vase
- Hera marker
- Circle stencil

TECHNIQUE TIP

When you score the second turning line of a ⅛"-wide bias stem, place the *inside* of the ⅛" ruler mark next to the first scored line. This will make up for the tiny bit of extra width that is added to your stem when you move the Hera marker next to the ruler.

STITCHING THE STEMS

1. Fold the background square diagonally in both directions to find the center point. Place the background square over the block pattern (page 43), matching center points. Trace the stem placement lines onto the background square.

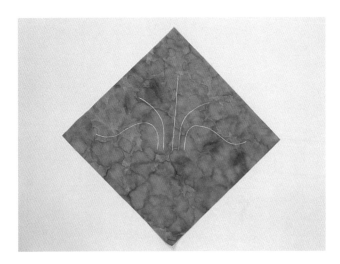

2. Referring to "Hera Bias Strips" on page 14, make five ⅛" x 6" bias stems. Referring to the directional stitching arrows shown on page 43, stitch the 5 stems onto the background square, trimming each to the correct length after you stitch the first edge.

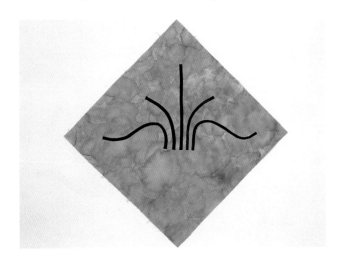

ADDING THE LEAVES

Trace the leaf shape (page 43) onto template plastic and cut it out. Mark around this template 18 times on the leaf fabrics and cut a ³⁄₁₆" seam allowance around each leaf. Stitch the leaves onto the stems as shown. Begin stitching each leaf near the stem so that you can make sure the points lie directly across from each other.

STITCHING THE DAFFODILS

1. Trace the lower and upper petals (page 43) onto template plastic and cut them out. Mark around the templates (15 lower petals and 15

upper petals) on a variety of fabrics in different colors, and cut a ³⁄₁₆" seam allowance around each shape. Place the petals on the 3 inner stems, experimenting with different color combinations until you create one that pleases you.

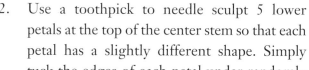

COLOR-BLENDING TIP

Choosing colors for flower petals is an opportunity to blend different colors together in the same flower. I used light, pale, clear colors for the lower petals that lie near the edges of my block so that they would look luminous against the dusty blue of my background fabric. For the other lower petals, I chose brighter colors, with values closer to that of my background fabric. Follow these guidelines—or better yet, let reality take a backseat to art, and allow your own color sense to take over. Enjoy coming up with unique color combinations.

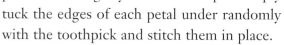

2. Use a toothpick to needle sculpt 5 lower petals at the top of the center stem so that each petal has a slightly different shape. Simply tuck the edges of each petal under randomly with the toothpick and stitch them in place.

3. Stitch the upper petals on top of the lower petals using the toothpick to needle sculpt these shapes as well. Repeat for all 3 flowers.

ADDING THE TRUMPET CENTERS

1. Using a circle stencil, mark a circle on the three 1½" squares of fabric for the rims of the trumpet centers. Choose whatever size circle you'd like for the opening in each trumpet center.

2. Mark a randomly curved line approximately ⅛" outside each marked circle. This is a quick way to create the rim for each trumpet center without using any templates. Cut a ³⁄₁₆" seam allowance around the curved edge of each rim.

3. Cut a seam allowance ³⁄₁₆" inside each circle. Clip the seam allowance, spacing each clip about ⅛" apart. Reverse appliqué each circle to a 2" square of fabric for the trumpet centers.

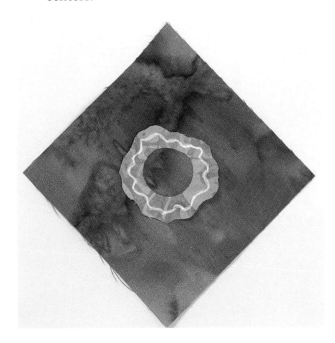

4. Lift the edges of each stitched circle and mark the trumpet center by drawing a shallow U shape from one side of your stitched circle to the other. Do this by eye so that each trumpet center has a slightly different curve.

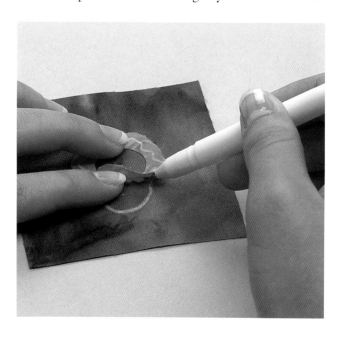

5. Cut a ³⁄₁₆" seam allowance around each U shape to complete the trumpet center units. Position and stitch the trumpet center units on your daffodils so that they face in any direction you like. They look great upside down, which makes the flower appear to face downward. They are also lovely when the trumpet centers face toward either side. Stitch the lower U shape first and finish by stitching around the rippled upper rim.

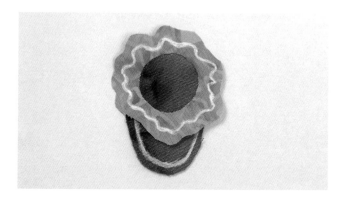

ADDING THE VASE

The fabric you choose for your vase can produce a variety of different effects. I used a dark batik print, with colors that echoed the yellows in my daffodils. Trace the vase pattern (page 43) onto template plastic and cut it out. Move the see-through template around on your fabric to determine where you wish to place the vase. Mark around the template and cut a ³⁄₁₆" seam allowance around the shape. Try cutting out a few vases from different fabrics and see which one you like best with your daffodils. Place and stitch the vase so that it covers the ends of the stems.

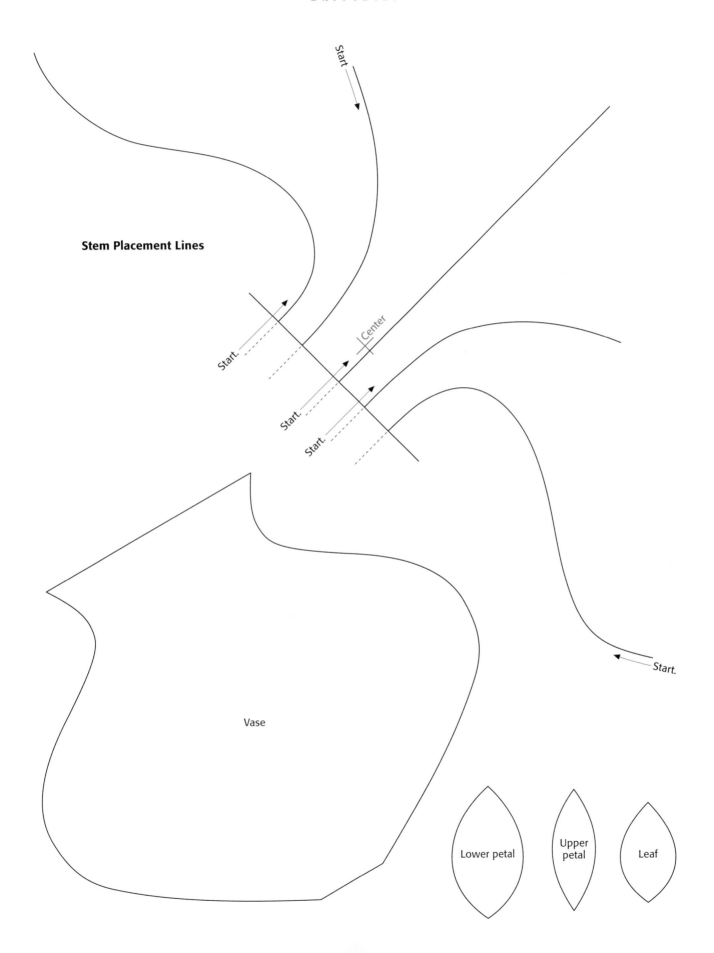

Start

Stem Placement Lines

Start.

Center

Start.

Start.

Start.

Vase

Lower petal

Upper petal

Leaf

ANTHURIUMS

With its shiny, heart-shaped blossoms, the Hawaiian anthurium is one of my favorite flowers. In this design, I color blended many fabrics in similar values together to create an artistic look that's true to the beauty of these elegant blossoms.

TECHNIQUES

Color blending (anthuriums)

Unit appliqué (anthuriums)

Using color to create luminosity (anthuriums)

Needle sculpting (curly willow branches)

Hera bias strips (stems)

Broderie perse appliqué (vase)

FABRICS AND SUPPLIES

- 11" square of fabric for background
- 6" square of fabric for stems
- Wide assortment of scrap fabrics for anthuriums
- 3" square of fabric for stamens
- 1 fat quarter of fabric for curly willow branches
- 8" square of fabric with medium-to-large motifs for vase
- 8" square of fabric for vase
- Hera marker

STITCHING THE STEMS

1. Fold the background square diagonally in both directions to find the center point. Place the background square over the block pattern (page 49), matching center points. Trace the stem placement lines onto the background square.

2. Referring to "Hera Bias Strips" on page 14, make three ⅛" x 4" bias stems. Stitch the 3 bias stems onto the background square, trimming each to the correct length after you stitch the first side.

COLOR-BLENDING TIP

On a flat surface, arrange a sequence of 11 to 15 fabrics in colors you'd like to use in your flowers, keeping the values fairly close. There are several ways to color blend each flower: start with darker fabrics and move gradually toward lighter ones, or vice versa. Or you can start with darks or lights in the middle and move toward the opposite value on either side. Refer to "Color Blending Fabrics" on page 17 for guidance and look through the quilts on pages 20–35 for more ideas. Let yourself be creative and play with many different color combinations. You can easily make changes and substitutions as you appliqué each anthurium.

STITCHING THE ANTHURIUMS

1. Trace the 3 anthurium patterns (page 49) onto freezer paper, extending the lines of each shape into each adjacent shape as shown. These little hatch marks will show you exactly where to begin and end stitching each shape to the next piece of fabric.

2. Cut out the first template at the tip of the flower and press it onto the fabric you have chosen for that shape. Mark around the template. Also make a small mark on the fabric to match each hatch mark on the template.

3. Remove the freezer paper and cut a ³⁄₁₆" seam allowance around the shape. Clip the fabric at each hatch mark up to the marked turning line.

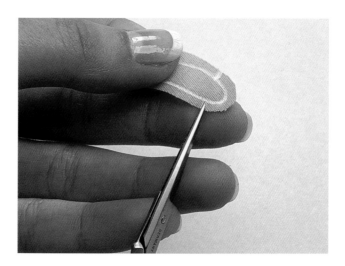

4. Starting at one clip and ending at the other, appliqué the first shape onto the fabric you have chosen for the second shape. This piece of fabric just needs to be large enough for the second shape with seam allowances.

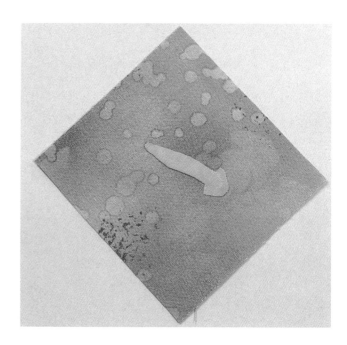

5. Cut out the second shape from the freezer paper and press it next to the stitched line on the first shape. Mark around the template and make small lines on the fabric to match the hatch marks on the template.

6. Remove the freezer paper and cut a ³⁄₁₆" seam allowance around the marked second shape. Clip the seam allowance at each hatch mark.

7. Repeat steps 4–6 to stitch each of the remaining shapes of the anthurium unit together, trimming the excess fabric underneath from the second shape onward. Repeat for the remaining 2 anthuriums.

8. Trace the stamen shapes (page 49) onto freezer paper and cut them out. Press them onto the stamen fabric, mark around them, and cut out each shape with a ³⁄₁₆" seam allowance. You will appliqué the stamens in place later, after the anthuriums are stitched to the background square.

STITCHING THE CURLY WILLOW BRANCHES

1. From the fabric for the curly willow branches, cut five ³⁄₈"-wide bias strips. Do *not* use a Hera marker to score turning lines on these strips.

2. To decide where you want to place your curly willow branches, start by pinning the anthurium units on the 3 stitched stems. Arrange the bias strips anywhere you like on your background fabric, making sure that the lower ends will fit inside the vase top after you stitch them. Trim some of the bias strips to shorter lengths, as desired, and position them

underneath the edges of your flowers. Pin the strips in place on the background fabric.

3. Appliqué each curly willow branch on the background square, allowing the edges to be uneven. Wherever you decide to create a dip in the branch, make a tiny clip (or more than one) into the bias strip. Then use a toothpick to needle sculpt the dip or V shape in the fabric as shown. There are no right or wrong ways to stitch curly willows—the more uneven they look, the more artistic your finished work will be.

4. Appliqué the anthuriums to the background square. Appliqué a stamen at the center of each anthurium.

ADDING THE VASE

1. To add a broderie perse motif to the vase, start by choosing a print fabric that features medium-to-large motifs. Cut out a shape that appeals to you, adding a ³⁄₁₆" seam allowance around it.

2. Stitch the motif onto a piece of fabric for the vase.

3. Trace the vase pattern (page 49) onto template plastic and cut it out. Move the see-through template over the stitched broderie

perse motif to determine where you wish to place the vase. Mark around the template.

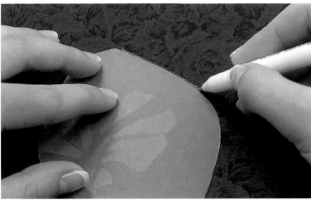

4. Cut a $\frac{3}{16}$" seam allowance around the vase unit. Trim the vase fabric under the stitched broderie perse motif to a $\frac{3}{16}$" seam allowance. Referring to the photo on page 44, stitch the vase on the background square, covering the ends of the stems and curly willow branches.

Stamen

Stamen

Center

Stamen

BEGONIA

A bright, multilayered flower anchors the center of this design, and the wide variety of leaves adds a hint of asymmetry. I used a much lighter version of the flower colors for the fleur-de-lis centers to make them look luminous.

TECHNIQUES

Reverse appliqué (fleur-de-lis units, large center circle)

Unit appliqué (begonia)

Hera bias strips (stems)

Inking (begonia)

Using color to create luminosity (fleur-de-lis centers)

Broderie perse appliqué (small center circle)

FABRICS AND SUPPLIES

- ◆ 10" square of fabric for fleur-de-lis units
- ◆ 10" square of fabric for fleur-de-lis centers
- ◆ Three 6" squares of fabric for begonia
- ◆ 2" square of fabric for large center circle
- ◆ 2" square of fabric with circle motifs for small center circle
- ◆ 23 (or more) assorted 2" squares of fabric for leaves
- ◆ 11" square of fabric for background
- ◆ 4" square of fabric for stems
- ◆ Circle stencil
- ◆ Hera marker
- ◆ Black (or other color) Pigma .01 mm marking pen for inking begonia

◆◆◆

COLOR-BLENDING TIP

Visit your local quilt shop and look for pate, clear fabrics that are either solid colors, tone-on-tone prints, or blended batiks. Fabrics like these are great for creating luminosity.

◆◆◆

STITCHING THE FLEUR-DE-LIS UNITS

1. Trace the fleur-de-lis unit patterns (page 56) onto freezer paper and cut them out. Press the freezer paper templates onto the fabric you've chosen for these shapes and mark around the inner and outer edges.

2. Remove the freezer paper and cut a ³⁄₁₆" seam allowance around the outer edge of each shape. Do not cut a seam allowance inside the inner marked lines at this time.

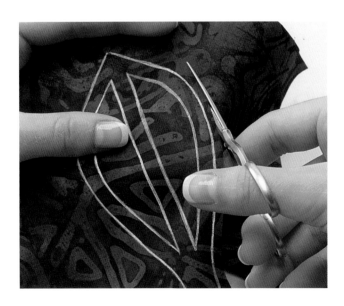

3. Place the piece of fabric for the fleur-de-lis centers underneath one of the outline shapes and pin the layers together. Begin cutting a ³⁄₁₆" seam allowance along one straight edge of the inner outline, taking care to cut only through the top layer of fabric. Trim some of the excess fabric, and begin reverse appliquéing the straight edge to the lower layer of fabric. Reverse appliqué the remaining inner portion of the outline shape to the lower layer of fabric.

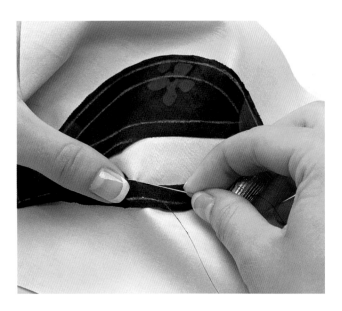

4. On the wrong side of your work, trim the lower layer to a ³⁄₁₆" seam allowance. Repeat steps 3 and 4 for the remaining fleur-de-lis units.

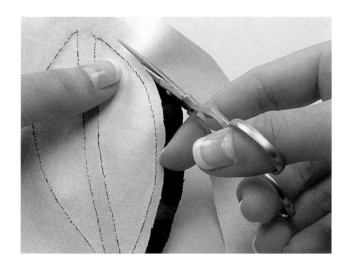

STITCHING THE BEGONIA

1. Trace the pattern for the top layer of the begonia (page 56) onto template plastic. Trace the pattern for the middle layer onto template plastic, filling in the missing lines to

make one shape. Do the same for the bottom layer and cut out all 3 templates.

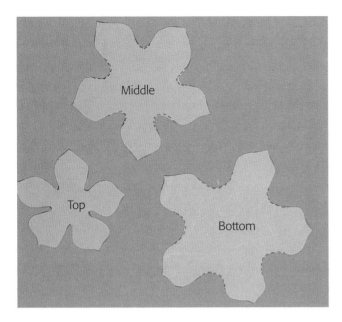

2. Place the top-layer template on a square of fabric for the top of the begonia and mark around it; remove the template. Use a circle stencil to mark a center circle just inside the petals of the top shape, or trace the circle pattern on page 56 onto template plastic and mark around it on the top shape. Cut a ³⁄₁₆" seam allowance around the top shape. Cut a ³⁄₁₆" seam allowance inside the center circle and make clips into the seam allowance about ⅛" apart.

3. Place the fabric for the large center circle underneath the top shape. Reverse appliqué the circle to the lower layer of fabric.

4. On the wrong side of your work, cut a ³⁄₁₆" seam allowance around the center circle.

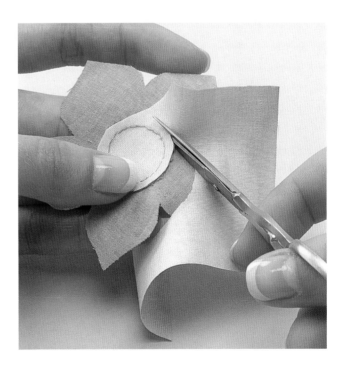

5. Place the middle-layer begonia template on a square of fabric for the middle of the begonia and mark around it; remove the template.

6. Appliqué the top begonia shape to the marked middle shape, beginning and ending each stitching line just inside the marked middle petals.

7. Cut a ³⁄₁₆" seam allowance around the middle shape. Trim the excess fabric underneath the top shape.

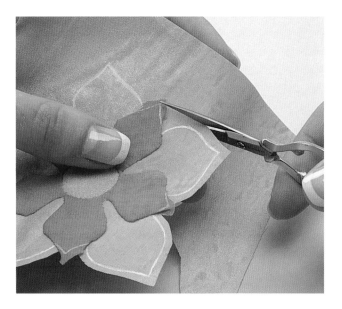

8. Mark around the bottom-layer begonia template on a piece of fabric for the bottom of the begonia. Stitch the top and middle shapes

to the marked bottom shape, beginning and ending each stitching line just inside the marked bottom petals.

9. Cut a ³⁄₁₆" seam allowance around the bottom shape and trim the excess fabric underneath the middle shape. Appliqué a small center circle cut from fabric with circle motifs on top of the large center circle.

PUTTING IT ALL TOGETHER

1. Trace the leaf pattern (page 56) onto template plastic and cut it out. Mark around this template 23 times on a variety of fabrics and cut a ³⁄₁₆" seam allowance around each leaf. Experiment with different colors and placements. You may prefer more or fewer leaves around your begonia.

2. Referring to the photo on page 50, arrange the begonia and fleur-de-lis units on the background square. Make sure that the begonia will overlap the edges of the fleur-de-lis units when stitched. Referring to "Hera Bias Strips" on page 14, make two ⅛" x 3" stems and place them on either side of the top of the begonia. Remove the begonia and fleur-de-lis units and stitch the stems in place.

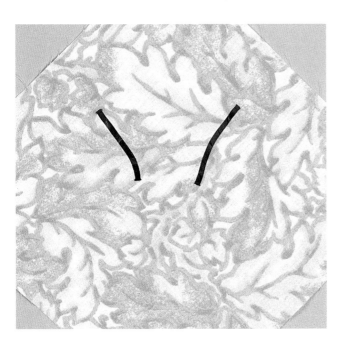

3. Appliqué the fleur-de-lis units in place. Place the begonia at the center and pin a selection of leaves around it, making sure that the begonia will overlap each of them when stitched. Also pin 3 leaves on each stem.

4. Remove the begonia and stitch the leaves in place. Appliqué the begonia over the leaves. Using a black (or other color) Pigma .01 mm marking pen, draw gently curved lines for stamens on the top petals, thickening the top of each line slightly. Add delicate, feathery lines on the lower petals.

TECHNIQUE TIP

After stitching 2 or 3 leaves, temporarily put the begonia in place again. This will help you decide whether you need to add more leaves, remove a few, or change the positions of leaves as needed.

Leaf

Bottom

Middle

Top

Center circle

Fleur-De-Lis Units

IRIS

Flowers are a never-ending inspiration for beautiful appliqué designs. Irises come in gorgeous colors and their rippled edges give each blossom a beauty all its own. Color blend your favorite hues together for this iris and let your color sense shine.

TECHNIQUES

Color blending (iris)

Sandwiching very thin strips of contrast color between narrow
    shapes (stamens)

Using color to create shadows (leaves)

Echoing colors (iris, leaves)

FABRICS AND SUPPLIES

- Wide assortment of scrap fabrics for iris
  petals
- 8" square of contrast fabric for stamens
- 8" square of fabric for stem, calyxes,
  and leaves
- 3" square of fabric for under-leaf
- 11" square of fabric for background

STITCHING THE IRIS

1. Trace the center and lower petal patterns
    (page 64) onto freezer paper, adding ½" to
    the areas that will lie underneath the center
    petal. Number the shapes as shown and cut
    the templates out.

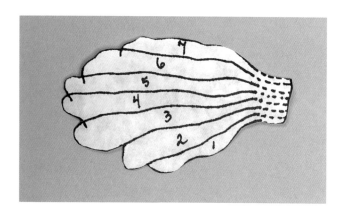

COLOR-BLENDING TIP

Look through gardening magazines and books on flower arranging for photos of irises. Notice which varieties and colors you find most appealing. Then arrange a sequence of 10 to 12 fabrics, including pastels, brights, mediums, and darks. All of these are great for color blending, as long as you keep the values similar between adjacent shapes. When you have an arrangement that pleases you, decide on a contrast color for the narrow stamens. You can use a single color or different ones, as long as there is high contrast with your iris fabrics.

2. Press the template for shape 1 of the lower-
    left petal onto a piece of fabric. Mark around
    it, remove the freezer paper, and cut a ³⁄₁₆"
    seam allowance around shape 1.

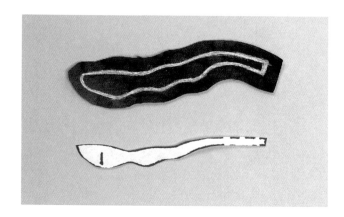

3. Stitch shape 1 to a piece of fabric for shape 2.

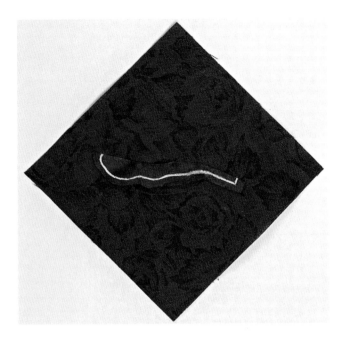

4. Press the template for shape 2 next to your stitched line on shape 1. Mark around the template.

5. Remove the freezer paper and cut a ³⁄₁₆" seam allowance around shape 2.

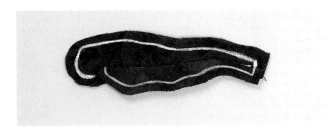

6. Repeat steps 3–5 to add shape 3.

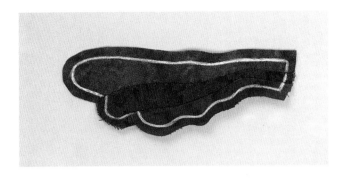

TECHNIQUE TIP

You can insert a narrow stamen between any two individual pieces in a color-blended flower petal.

7. Stitch just a portion of shape 3 to a piece of contrast fabric for stamens. This stitched line should be as long as you want your finished stamen to be. This is a free-form technique—there is no right or wrong length for each stamen. Let your creative juices flow.

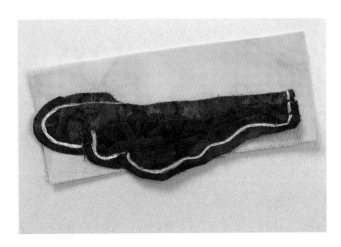

8. Trim the contrast stamen fabric to ¼" from your stitched line, taking care also to leave about ¼" of fabric beyond the end of your stitching line. Also trim the stamen fabric underneath the petal unit.

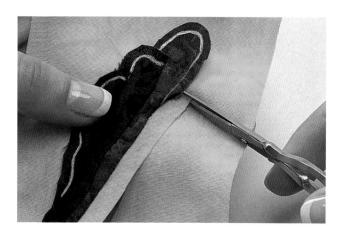

9. Make clips into the contrast stamen fabric to make it easy to turn under. Space these clips about ¼" apart, and cut to ⅛" from the stitched line. Fold the contrast fabric under and finger-press it so that only a narrow portion is visible. Let this fold be slightly uneven so the finished stamen will have a natural look. Treating the contrast fabric and iris fabric of shape 3 as a single stitching line, stitch them onto a piece of fabric for shape 4. Mark shape 4 as shown.

10. Continue adding petal shapes and inserting stamens in the same manner to complete the lower-left petal.

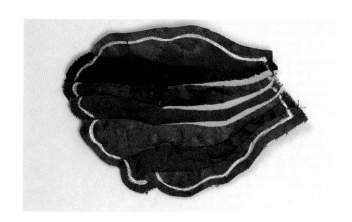

TECHNIQUE TIP

Because unit appliqué is so forgiving, it is easy to make any adjustments necessary as you press each template next to the stitched line of a previous shape. Keep in mind that your iris petals do not need to be identical to mine. Each flower you stitch with this technique should be a reflection of your own creativity.

11. Repeat steps 1–10 to appliqué the shapes in the center and lower-right petals.

12. Trace the 2 top petals (page 64) onto freezer paper, allowing ½" for the areas that will lie underneath the center petal. Cut shape 1 from the template, press it onto a piece of fabric, and mark around it. Remove the freezer paper and cut a ³⁄₁₆" seam allowance around the shape. Stitch shape 1 to a piece of fabric for shape 2. Cut and press the template for shape 2 next to your stitched line. Mark around it, remove the freezer paper, and cut a ³⁄₁₆" seam allowance around the edge. Repeat for shape 3.

13. Repeat step 12 to make the second top petal.

STITCHING THE STEM AND CALYXES

1. Trace the stem and calyx patterns (page 64) onto freezer paper and cut them out. Label the top and middle calyxes.

2. Set aside the top and middle calyx templates temporarily. Press the stem template onto the stem fabric, mark around it, remove the freezer paper, and cut a ³⁄₁₆" seam allowance around the stem shape. Clip the curved seam allowance at the top of the stem, spacing the clips ⅛" apart. Stitch this curved edge to the stem fabric for the middle calyx.

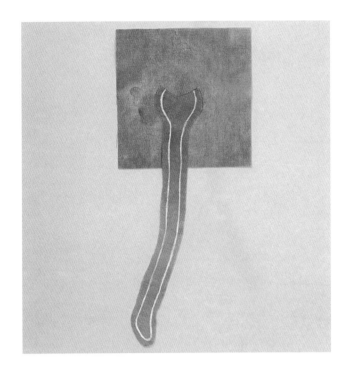

3. Press the middle calyx template next to the stitched line and mark around it. Remove the freezer paper and cut a ³⁄₁₆" seam allowance around the middle calyx.

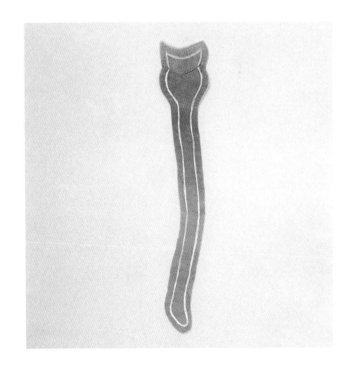

4. Press the template for the top calyx on the stem fabric. Mark only the curved edge at the top and extend this line ½" on either side.

5. Remove the top calyx template temporarily, and cut a ³⁄₁₆" seam allowance along the marked curve. Clip this seam allowance at ⅛" intervals and stitch this edge over your center petal unit. The extended lines on the top calyx will enable you to custom-fit it to the width of your center petal unit. Press the top calyx template next to your stitched line on the center petal unit and mark around it; remove the freezer paper.

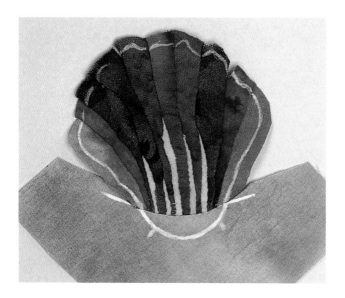

6. Then stitch the middle calyx in place. Cut a ³⁄₁₆" seam allowance at the sides of the top calyx and trim the excess fabric underneath to a ³⁄₁₆" seam allowance.

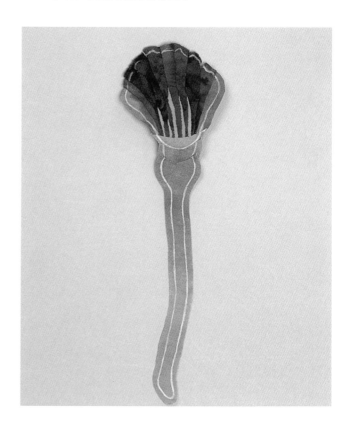

STITCHING THE LEAVES

1. Trace the 2-part leaf shape (page 64) onto freezer paper, adding a hatch mark where the under-leaf shape meets the top-leaf shape. Cut the 2 shapes apart. Press the top-leaf template onto a piece of fabric and mark around it, including the hatch mark. Remove the freezer paper and cut a ³⁄₁₆" seam allowance around the top-leaf shape. Clip the seam allowance at the hatch mark and stitch the

top-leaf shape to a piece of fabric for the under-leaf shape.

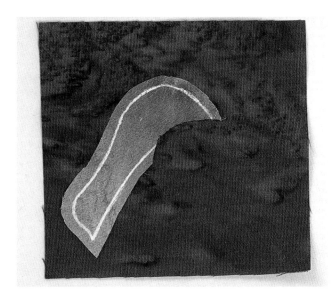

2. Press the under-leaf template next to your stitched line and mark around it. Remove the freezer paper and cut a ³⁄₁₆" seam allowance around the under-leaf shape.

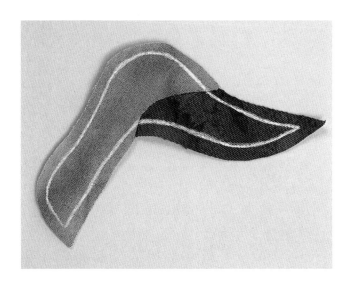

3. Trace the remaining leaf shapes (page 64) onto freezer paper and cut them out. Press the shapes onto the leaf fabric and mark around them. Remove the freezer paper and cut a ³⁄₁₆" seam allowance around them.

COLOR-BLENDING TIPS

For the under-leaf, use a darker, grayed shade of your top-leaf color. This will make the under-leaf look as if it is in shadow, enhancing its three-dimensional appearance.

You can use color to create a feeling of continuity by repeating certain hues in different parts of an appliqué design. In this block, I chose a green-and-lavender hand-painted fabric from Skydyes for the stem, calyxes, and leaves, to echo the purples in my iris.

PUTTING IT ALL TOGETHER

1. Pin the 2 top petal units, the 2 side petal units, and the center petal unit with the stem and calyx on your background fabric. When you have positioned each unit where you like, remove the center petal and stem, and stitch the 2 side and 2 top petal units in place.

2. Stitch the center petal unit with stem and calyx in position over the top and side petal units.

3. Stitch the 3 leaves next to the stem.

ORCHID

Orchids have a lush beauty that is truly exotic. Try experimenting with lots of different color combinations for the petals and flower center. There are no right or wrong ways to use color in this design—let your own color preferences have free rein.

TECHNIQUES

Unit appliqué (orchid, 2-part leaves)

Inking (petals)

Using color to create luminosity (petals)

Broderie perse appliqué (center circle)

FABRICS AND SUPPLIES

- Two 4" squares of fabric for upper-side petals
- Scraps of fabric for under-areas of upper-side petals
- Assorted scraps of fabric for bottom petal
- Three 4" squares of fabric for top and lower-side petals
- 4" square of fabric for flower center
- Scrap of fabric with circle motifs for center circle
- Assorted scraps of fabric for leaves and tendrils
- 6" square of fabric for vase
- 11" square of fabric for background
- Brown (or other color) Pigma .01 mm marking pen for inking orchid

STITCHING THE UPPER-SIDE PETALS

1. Trace the 2 upper-side petals (page 70) onto freezer paper, adding ½" to the edges that will lie underneath the flower center. Include

hatch marks wherever an underneath area will be visible in the finished petals. Do not mark the lines of these under-areas; you can mark these lines by eye later.

2. Cut out the upper-side petal templates and press them onto pieces of fabric. Mark around each template, including the hatch marks. Remove the freezer paper and cut a ³⁄₁₆" seam allowance around each shape. Stitch the upper-side petals to fabric for the under-areas, beginning and ending each seam line at a hatch mark. Mark a short line that goes from one end of your stitched line to the other as shown.

COLOR-BLENDING TIP

If you choose a dark background fabric, use a pale color to make the orchid petals appear to glow. If your background fabric is light, use bright or dark colors to give your orchid a dramatic look.

3. Cut a ³⁄₁₆" seam allowance around each of the under-areas on each upper-side petal.

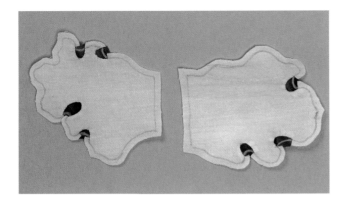

STITCHING THE BOTTOM PETAL

1. Trace the bottom petal shape (page 70) onto freezer paper, including the hatch marks and adding ½" to the edge that will lie underneath the center circle. Number the shapes as indicated and cut the template out.

2. Cut shape 1 from the template and press it on a piece of fabric. Mark around the template, including the hatch mark. Remove the freezer paper and cut a ³⁄₁₆" seam allowance around the shape.

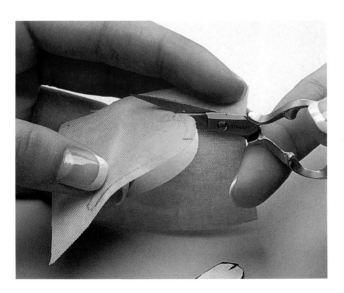

3. Clip the seam allowance at the hatch mark and stitch shape 1 to a piece of fabric for shape 2. Cut shape 2 from the template and press it next to the stitched line. Mark around the template, including the hatch mark.

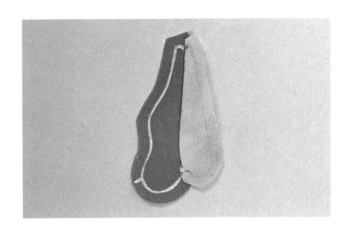

4. Remove the freezer paper and cut a ³⁄₁₆" seam allowance around shape 2.

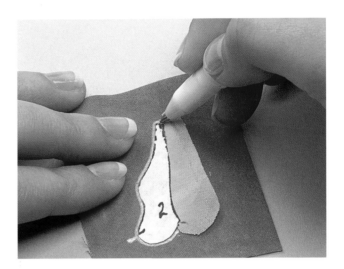

5. Continue adding shapes in the same manner to complete the bottom petal unit.

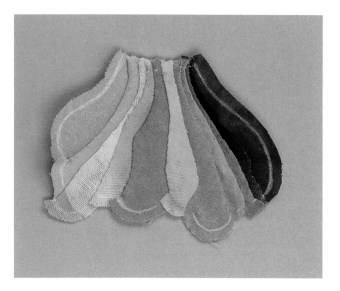

ASSEMBLING THE ORCHID

1. Trace the top petal and the 2 lower-side petals (page 70) onto freezer paper, adding ½" to the edges that will lie underneath the flower center. Trace the flower center, adding ½" to the edge that will lie underneath the bottom petal unit. Cut the templates out and press them onto pieces of fabric. Mark around the templates, remove the freezer paper, and cut a ³⁄₁₆" seam allowance around each shape.

2. On a flat surface, arrange the top petal, the 2 upper-side petal units, the 2 lower-side petals, the flower center, and the bottom petal unit as you wish, and pin them together. Stitch the flower center to the upper-side petals, beginning and ending these stitching lines inside the marked lines of the upper-side petals. In

the same manner, stitch the flower center to the top petal and the 2 lower-side petals.

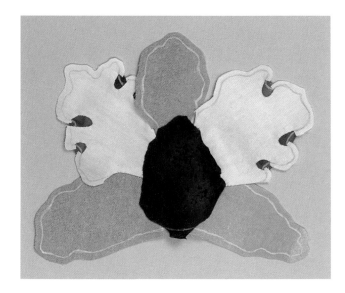

3. Stitch the bottom petal unit over the lower edge of the flower center, and appliqué a small center circle cut from fabric with circle motifs to the top of the bottom petal unit. Using a brown Pigma .01 mm marking pen, draw faint, feathery lines on the top petal, the upper-side petals, and the lower-side petals.

TECHNIQUE TIP

If the thought of inking your finished appliqué seems daunting, try this trick. After you finish stitching the block, make several black-and-white photocopies of it and practice inking different lines and curves on the photocopies. Experiment with lighter or softer pressure on your pen, and try various curves and lines on each petal. When you are happy with the effects you've created on paper, use it as a guide to inking the fabric.

STITCHING THE 2-PART LEAVES

1. Trace the 2-part leaf shapes (page 70) onto freezer paper and cut out the templates. Cut the inner leaf shape from each template and press them onto fabric. Mark around the templates, remove the freezer paper, and cut a ³⁄₁₆" seam allowance around the shapes. Stitch the inner leaf shapes to a piece of fabric for the other half of the leaves. Press the remaining leaf templates next to your stitched lines and mark around them.

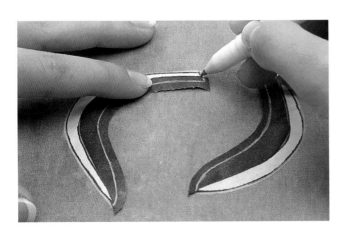

2. Remove the freezer paper and cut a ³⁄₁₆" seam allowance around each 2-part leaf unit.

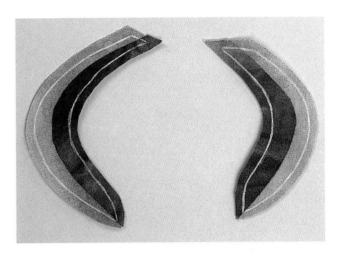

PUTTING IT ALL TOGETHER

1. Trace the leaf and tendril shapes (page 70) onto freezer paper, adding ½" to the edges that will lie underneath the orchid. Cut the templates out and press them onto fabric. Mark around them, remove the freezer paper, and cut a ³⁄₁₆" seam allowance around each shape.

2. Trace the vase shape (page 70) onto freezer paper. Cut the template out and press it onto a piece of vase fabric. Mark around the shape, remove the freezer paper, and cut a ³⁄₁₆" seam allowance around it.

3. Arrange the vase, leaves, tendrils, 2-part leaf units, and orchid unit on the background square. When you have an arrangement that pleases you, remove the orchid unit and stitch the leaves, tendrils, and vase in place. Then stitch the orchid unit in place.

HIBISCUS

Free-form appliqué allows you to needle sculpt the edges of an appliqué shape any way you like. The starting point for each of the five petals in this flower is a single narrow center shape. From there, it's easy to build outward on either side, adding more narrow shapes until each petal is the size you want it to be. This technique lets you "grow" your flowers—there are no marked turning lines to follow.

TECHNIQUES

Color blending (hibiscus)
Reverse appliqué (background)
Needle sculpting (hibiscus)
Echoing colors (hibiscus, leaves)

FABRICS AND SUPPLIES

◆ 11" square of dark fabric for background

◆ 11" square of light or medium fabric for background

◆ Wide assortment of scrap fabrics for hibiscus petals

◆ 6" square of fabric for center leaves

◆ 3" square of fabric for flower center

◆ Scrap of fabric with circle motifs for center circle

◆ Wide assortment of scrap fabrics for outer leaves

STITCHING THE BACKGROUND SQUARE

1. Using a permanent marking pen, draw an 11" square on a piece of freezer paper. Inside this

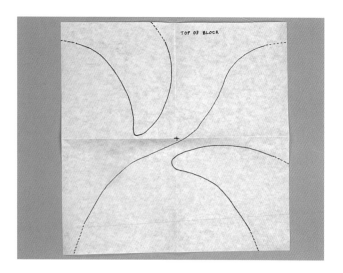

square, trace the lines of the background pattern (page 78), extending the lines to meet the edges of the square.

2. Cut out the curved areas indicated on the square background template and cut the background template in half along the diagonal curved line. Press the right half of the background template onto the 11" square of dark background fabric. Mark along the lines and cut a ³⁄₁₆" seam allowance next to each line as shown. Then remove the freezer paper. Reserve the trimmed portion of fabric; you will need it later to appliqué the curved area at the upper-left corner of the background.

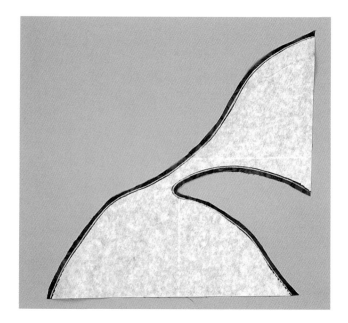

3. Press the left half of the background template onto the 11" square of light background fabric. Mark around the curved line at the top (omit the diagonal curved line) and cut a seam

allowance ³⁄₁₆" from the marked line. Then remove the freezer paper.

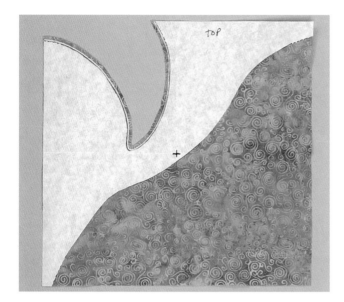

4. Layer the dark background fabric marked with the curved diagonal line and lower curved area on top of the light background square. Make sure the curved area on the light background square is positioned in the upper-left corner. Appliqué the curved diagonal line of the dark fabric. Reverse appliqué the curved area in the lower-right corner. Layer the trimmed portion of the dark fabric from step 2 underneath cut-out curved area at the upper left of the light background square.

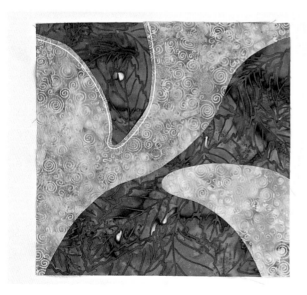

5. Reverse appliqué the curve at the upper-left corner. On the wrong side of your work, trim a ³⁄₁₆" seam allowance from the stitched lines. Press the completed background square.

COLOR-BLENDING TIP

Arrange a sequence of fabrics in the colors you'd like to use for your hibiscus. Referring to "Color Blending Fabrics" on page 17, choose a wide selection of fabrics. You can create the look of light shining on a flower by using pastel colors in some areas and slightly darker colors in others, as long as you keep the values similar between neighboring colors. For the hibiscus in my block, I used cream, white, pale lavender, yellow, blue, gray, pink, and coral to create the overall effect of a pastel pink flower.

STITCHING THE PETAL UNITS

1. Trace the angled lines and curve (page 79) onto a piece of freezer paper.

2. The narrow petal shape (page 79) is the center shape in each of the 5 petal units of the hibiscus. Trace this shape onto template plastic and cut it out. Mark the shape on a piece of fabric and cut it out *on* the marked lines (no seam allowance). Stitch the right edge of this shape to a piece of fabric in a similar value for shape 2, using a toothpick to needle sculpt the edge unevenly. Make clips into the fabric wherever you wish to make it easier to create an irregular edge.

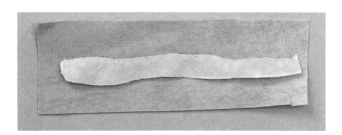

3. Trim the fabric for shape 2 to approximately ¼" from the stitched line. There is no need to mark a turning line on the second shape. Each shape in this free-form hibiscus should be slightly different and shaped by the toothpick as you go. Make each shape wider at the top, sloping down to a very narrow width at the bottom.

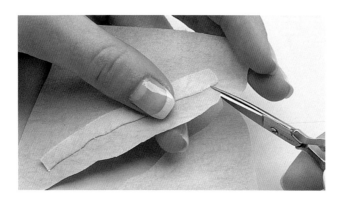

4. Stitch the left edge of the center shape to another piece of fabric. Turn the fabric under farther at the base to give the petal a fan-like shape, and keep the values of the fabrics similar.

5. In the same manner, cut this shape to approximately ¼" from your stitched line.

6. Continue adding shapes on both sides of the center shape in the same manner. When you have stitched together 10 to 13 narrow shapes, lay them between 2 of the angled lines; this will show you whether you need to continue adding more shapes to the petal or not.

7. When the tops of your petal reach the curved line and fill the space between 2 angled lines, the petal will be approximately the correct width and height.

8. Stitch 4 more petals together in the same manner. Pin the 5 completed petal units between the angled lines.

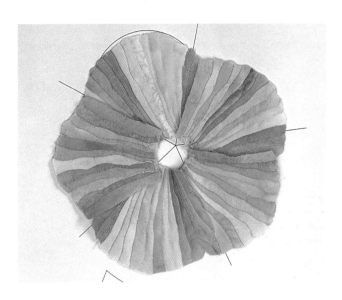

TECHNIQUE TIP

This free-form appliqué technique is very forgiving. If you find that you have added too many shapes to one petal, you can simply turn under as much of the petal as necessary.

JOINING THE PETAL UNITS

1. Keeping the angle between 2 petal units the same as it was on the freezer paper, stitch the edges of the petal units to a piece of fabric to join them into a circle.

2. Trim the fabric that joins the 2 petal units, and place the 2 joined petals back on the freezer paper to check the angle of each shape. You can always add another petal or petals to either end of the joined petal shapes to make them fill out the curved area on the paper, if necessary.

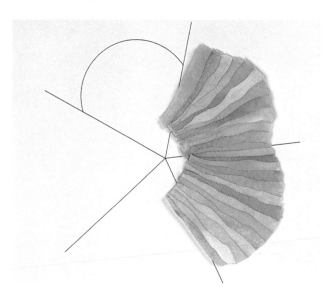

3. Repeat steps 1 and 2 to join each of the remaining petal units, comparing the joined petal units to the angled lines on the freezer paper after joining each pair of petal units. There will be a small opening at the center of the completed hibiscus, which will be covered later by the center leaves.

STITCHING THE FLOWER CENTER

1. Trace the center leaf shape and flower center shape (page 79) onto freezer paper and cut them out. Mark the flower center shape and 5 center leaves on the appropriate fabrics. Remove the freezer paper and cut a ³⁄₁₆" seam allowance around each shape.

2. Referring to the photo on page 71, stitch the center leaves in place at the center of the hibiscus. Stitch the flower center on top of the center leaves. Add a small center circle cut from fabric with circle motifs.

PUTTING IT
ALL TOGETHER

1. Trace the outer leaf shape (page 79) onto template plastic and cut it out. Mark around this template on a wide variety of different fabrics and cut a ³⁄₁₆" seam allowance around each leaf.

2. Pin the completed hibiscus unit at the center of the background square and add leaves all around it.

3. When you are happy with your arrangement, remove the hibiscus unit temporarily and stitch the leaves in place. After every 2 or 3 leaves you stitch, place the hibiscus unit in position again to make sure that all of your leaves will lie underneath the hibiscus when stitched.

COLOR-BLENDING TIP

For the lighter areas in your background square, choose darker leaves for greater contrast. In the darker areas of your background square, place lighter or brighter leaves.

4. Stitch the hibiscus unit in place over the leaves.

Background Pattern

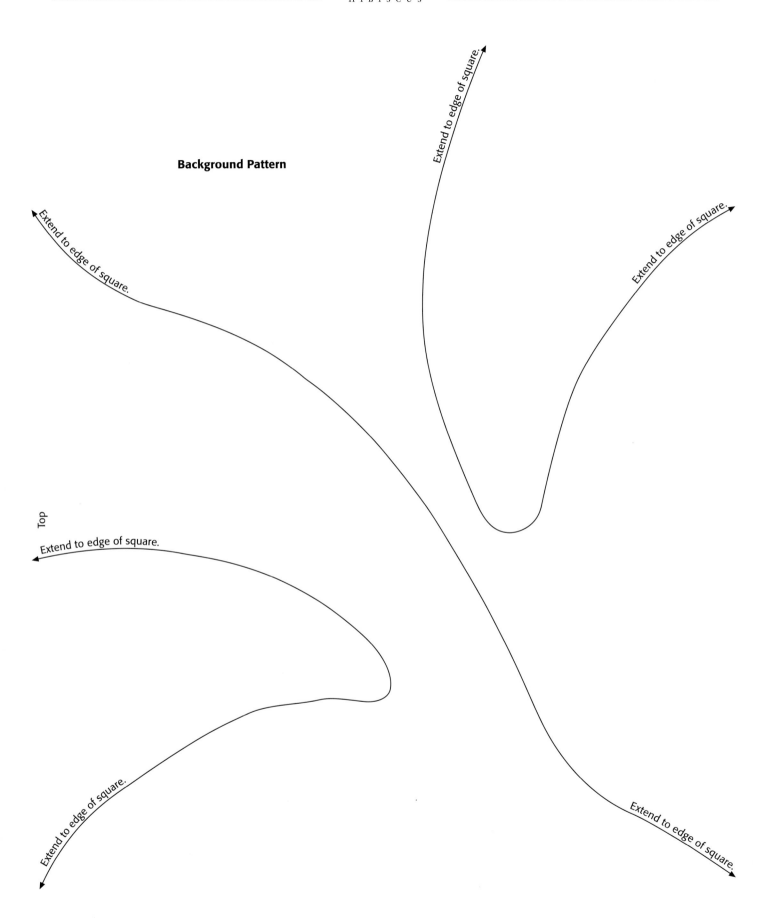

Extend to edge of square.

Extend to edge of square.

Extend to edge of square.

Top

Extend to edge of square.

Extend to edge of square.

Extend to edge of square.

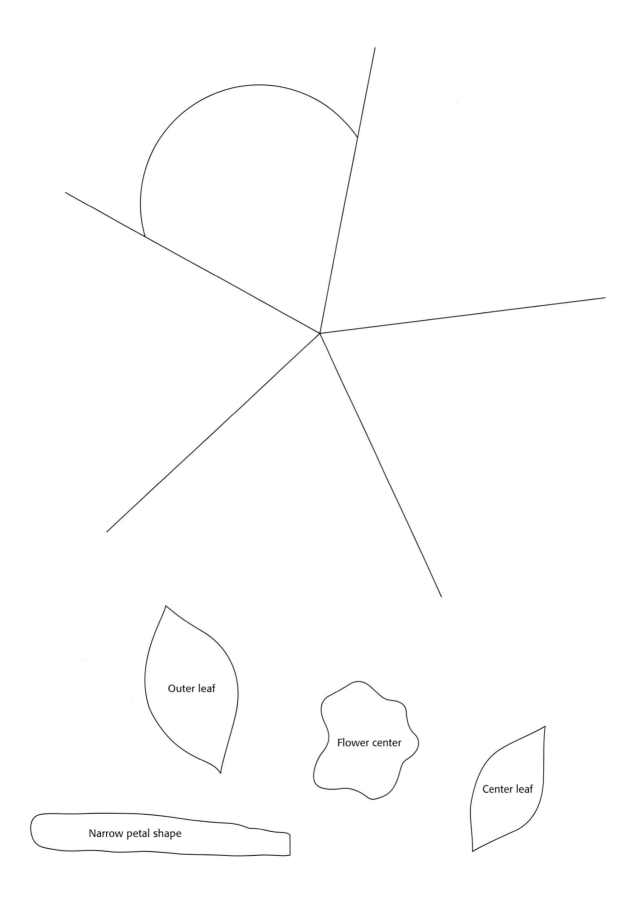

Outer leaf

Flower center

Center leaf

Narrow petal shape

CALLA LILY

"Elegant" is the best word to describe a calla lily; its long, graceful stems and blossoms are sleek, simple, and refined. Color blend your favorite hues for the stems, the leaf, and the bottom of the lily, and add accents of cotton or tissue lamé in any color you like.

TECHNIQUES

Color blending (stems, base of lily)

Needle sculpting (stems)

Using lamé (lily, leaf)

Inking to create shadows (lily)

Sandwiching very thin strips of contrast color between narrow shapes (leaf)

FABRICS AND SUPPLIES

- Three 9" squares of fabric for stems
- Assorted scrap fabrics for leaf
- Two 3" squares of fabric for stamen
- 6" square of fabric for top of lily
- Assorted scrap fabrics for bottom of lily
- 6" square of cotton or tissue lamé for lily and leaf accents
- 6" square of fusible tricot interfacing
- 11" square of fabric for background
- Black, brown, pink, and orange (or other colors) Pigma .01 mm marking pens for inking lily

◆◆◆

COLOR-BLENDING TIP

You can color blend any appliqué shape, even if it is only ¼" wide, such as the stems in this design. Choose 3 compatible colors, keeping the values of the 2 outer-edge fabrics very similar and selecting a third fabric that is lighter and/or brighter for the middle of the stem. Investigate tone-on-tone batiks for the outer 2 fabrics and multicolored batiks for the middle fabric.

◆◆◆

STITCHING THE STEMS

1. Trace the stem patterns (page 87) onto freezer paper and cut them out. Note that these patterns have parallel edges; you will shape the stems randomly as you stitch them.

2. Press the longest stem template onto a piece of fabric for the left edge of the stem. Mark around it, remove the freezer paper, and cut the stem out on the marked lines (no seam allowance).

3. Stitch the lower-right portion of the stem to a piece of fabric for the middle area of the stem. Wherever necessary, clip the seam allowance and use a toothpick to needle sculpt the edge irregularly as you go. Trim the fabric to ¼" from your stitched line.

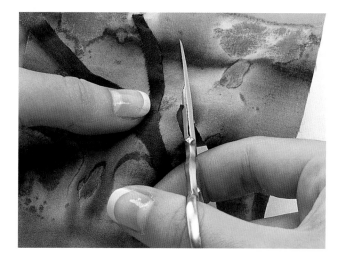

4. Turn under and finger-crease an irregular fold in the middle fabric, approximately ⅛" from the stitched line. Clip the fabric as necessary to help create an uneven edge, and stitch the middle fabric to a piece of fabric for the right edge of the stem.

5. Trim the fabric for the right edge of the stem to ¼".

6. Repeat steps 3–5 to stitch the upper-left portion of the long stem and the 2 shorter stems.

STITCHING THE LEAF

1. Trace the leaf pattern (page 87) onto freezer paper, numbering the stitching sequence as indicated, and cut it out.

TECHNIQUE TIP

To help make accurate clips into tiny seam allowances, try stabilizing the underneath blade of your scissors by positioning its tip on the ring finger of your left hand. (Reverse this if you are left-handed.)

---

2. Cut shape 1 from the leaf template. Press it onto a piece of fabric and mark around it. Remove the freezer paper, cut a $3/16$" seam allowance around shape 1, and stitch the short side to a piece of contrasting fabric for the narrow band of color between shape 1 and shape 2. Trim the fabric to $1/4$" from your stitched line. Make clips in the fabric to $1/8$" from the stitched line, spacing them approximately $1/8$" to $1/4$" apart.

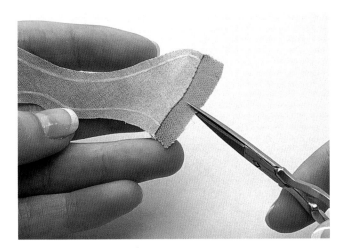

3. Turn under and stitch the contrast fabric to a piece of fabric for shape 2, shaping the fabric irregularly and allowing only a narrow band of it to show. Cut shape 2 from the leaf template and press it next to shape 1, *overlapping* the narrow band of color. Mark around it, remove the freezer paper, and cut a $3/16$" seam allowance around shape 2.

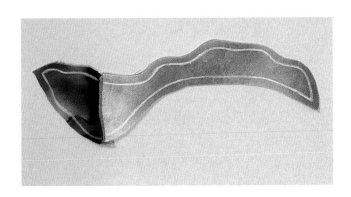

4. Continue adding the remaining shapes to the leaf unit in the same manner, inserting narrow bands of color as desired.

PREPARING THE STAMEN

1. Trace the stamen pattern (page 87) onto freezer paper and cut it out. Press the stamen template onto a piece of fabric. Mark around it, remove the freezer paper, and cut a ³⁄₁₆" seam allowance around the stamen.

2. Stitch the stamen to a piece of fabric for the outer edges of the stamen. Trim the fabric to approximately ¼" from the stitched line.

STITCHING THE CALLA LILY

1. Trace the calla lily pattern (page 87) onto freezer paper, numbering the stitching sequence of the bottom-right portion as indicated, and cut the template out. Note that you do not need to trace the areas labeled "lamé"; these edges will be stitched randomly.

2. Cut the top portion of the calla lily from the template and press it onto a piece of fabric. Mark around the template and remove the freezer paper.

3. Stitch the stamen unit to the lily top, shaping the edges randomly as you go. Cut a ³⁄₁₆" seam allowance around the lily top.

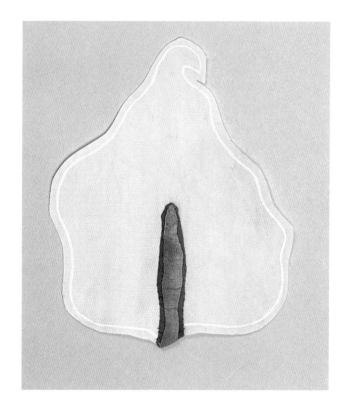

4. Stitch the lower-left and upper-right edges of the lily top to a piece of cotton or tissue lamé, referring to the photo on page 80. Trim the lamé to ¼" from the stitched lines.

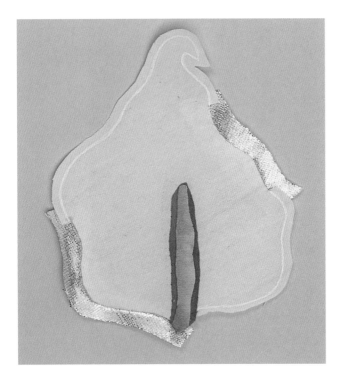

5. Cut shape 1 from the bottom-right portion of the lily template and press it onto a piece of fabric. Mark around it, remove the freezer paper, and cut a ³/16" seam allowance around the shape. Stitch shape 1 to a piece of fabric for shape 2.

6. Cut shape 2 from the template and press it next to your stitched line. Mark around it, remove the freezer paper, and cut a ³/16" seam allowance around shape 2.

7. Continue adding shapes in the same manner until the bottom-right lily unit is completed. Stitch the left edge of this unit to a piece of lamé and trim the lamé to ¼" from your stitched line.

8. Mark the lower-left portion of the bottom lily shape on fabric. Cut it out with a ³⁄₁₆" seam allowance on the left side and a ¼" seam allowance on the right and top edges. Stitch the lower-left edge of the lily top to the lower-left portion of the bottom lily shape. Take care as you turn under the lamé, and make as few clips as possible to avoid fraying this delicate fabric.

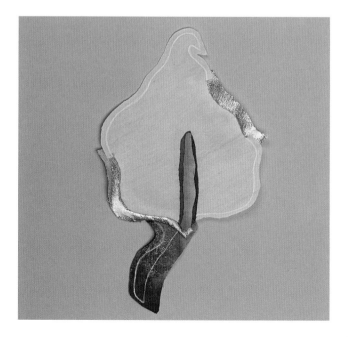

9. Stitch the edge of the bottom-right lily unit over the lily top and lower-left lily bottom. Take care as you turn under the lamé, and make as few clips as possible.

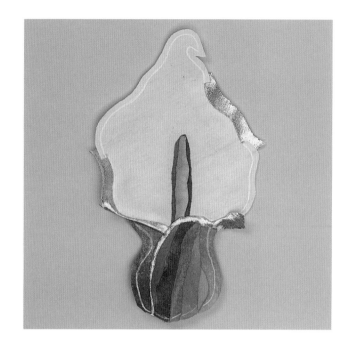

PUTTING IT ALL TOGETHER

1. Arrange the stems, leaf unit, and lily unit on the background square, referring to the photo on page 80. When you are happy with your arrangement, stitch the stems, followed by the leaf unit and the lily unit.

2. Using Pigma .01 mm marking pens in black, brown, pink, and orange (or other colors of your choice), add stippling around the stamen on the lily top. Use the darker colors nearest the stamen, and use lighter colors as you move toward the edges of the lily top.

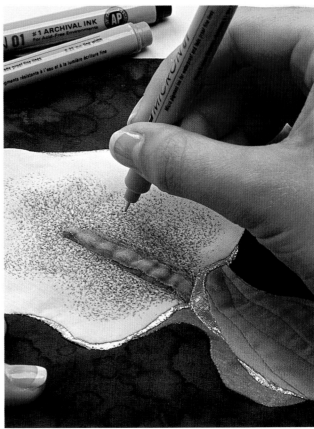

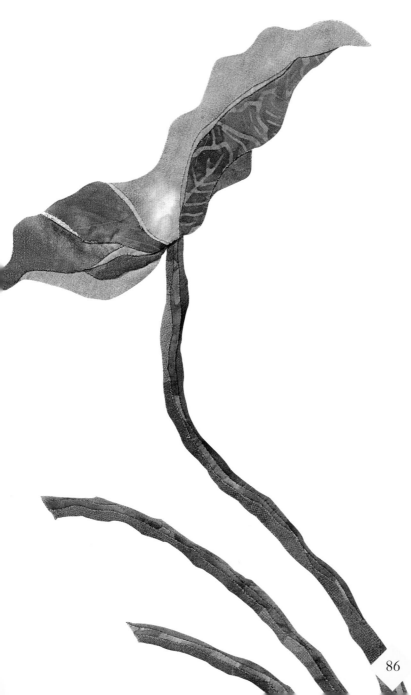

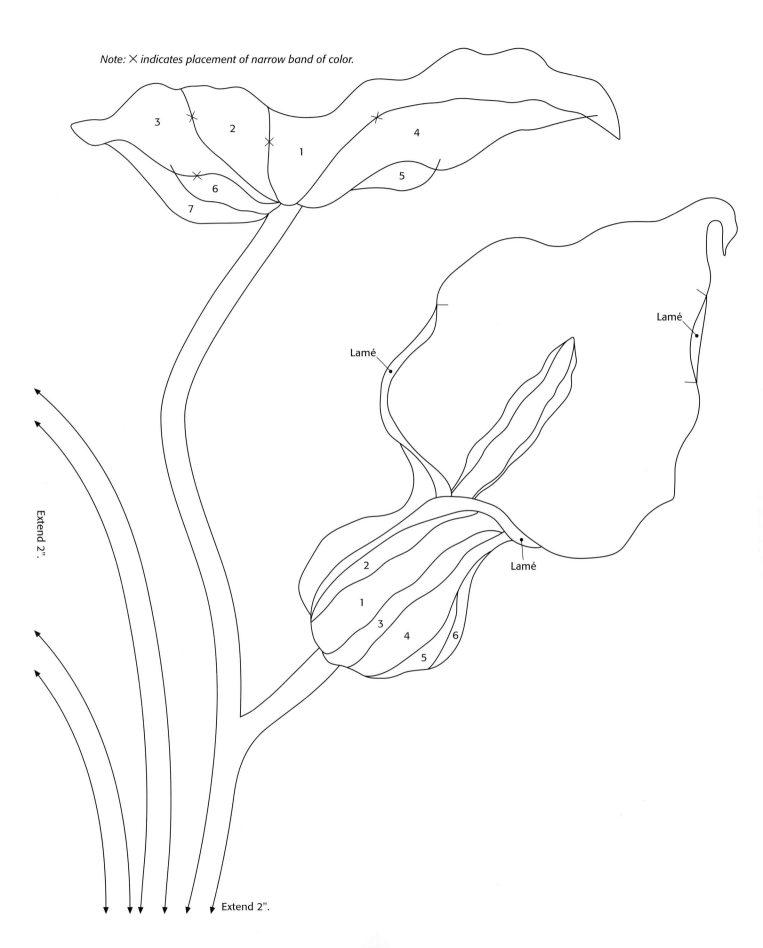

Note: ✕ indicates placement of narrow band of color.

3

2

1

4

5

6

7

Lamé

Lamé

Lamé

2

1

3

4

5

6

Extend 2".

Extend 2".

POPPIES

Imagine a field of colorful poppies swaying gently in a breeze, sunlight and shadow making the colors shimmer and blend in an ever-shifting pattern. Hold that image in your mind as you color blend fabrics for your poppies.

TECHNIQUES

Color blending (poppies)

Reverse appliqué with silk (leaf, poppies)

Three-dimensional stamens (poppies)

Inking (large poppy)

Needle sculpting (poppies)

FABRICS AND SUPPLIES

- 11" square of fabric for background
- 6" square of fabric for under-leaf (silk or silk douppioni, if desired)
- 9" square of fabric for stem and leaf top
- Wide assortment of scrap fabrics for poppies
- 6" square of fabric for back of large poppy (silk or silk douppioni, if desired)
- 4" square of fabric for back of small poppy (silk or silk douppioni, if desired)
- 6" square of lightweight fusible tricot interfacing (optional)
- Three-dimensional stamens (optional; available at craft and floral supply stores)
- Black (or other color) Pigma .01 mm marking pen for inking large poppy

STITCHING THE STEM AND LEAF

1. Trace the under-leaf pattern (page 93) onto freezer paper, connecting the dashed lines to create a single shape, and cut it out. Also trace and cut out the stem and leaf-top pattern. To position the under-leaf on your background square, fold the background square diagonally in both directions to find the center point. Open up the fabric and position the 2 templates on the background square, referring to the photo on page 88.

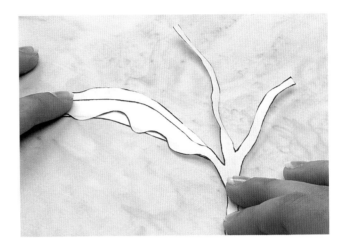

2. Press the under-leaf template in place on the background fabric and mark around it. Remove the freezer paper, cut a ³⁄₁₆" seam allowance *inside* the marked shape, and reverse appliqué the background fabric to a lower layer of fabric for the under-leaf. Press the stitched under-leaf shape to prepare it for stitching the stem and leaf top in place.

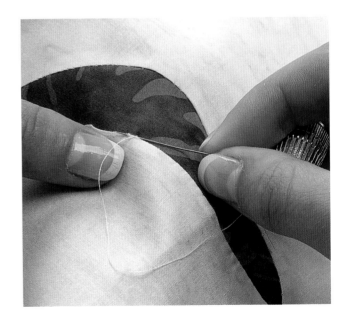

3. Press the stem-and-leaf-top template onto a piece of fabric and mark around it. Remove the freezer paper and cut a $^3/_{16}$" seam allowance around the shape. Stitch it on top of the stitched under-leaf, starting in the angle where the leaf top meets the stem. This will allow you to make sure that the leaf top will overlap the bottom of the under-leaf correctly when stitched.

STITCHING THE POPPIES

1. Trace the front part of the large poppy (page 93) onto freezer paper. Cut out the center shape and press it onto a piece of fabric. Mark around it, remove the freezer paper, and cut a $^3/_{16}$" seam allowance around it.

2. Stitch the right edge of the first shape to a piece of fabric for the adjacent shape.

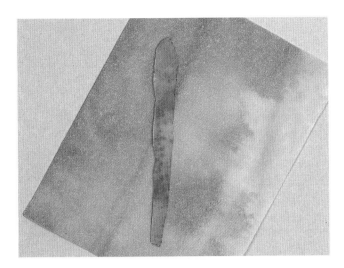

3. Cut a second petal shape randomly from the fabric, shaping it so that it is wider at the top than at the bottom.

4. Repeat steps 2 and 3 on the other side of the center shape and continue adding randomly shaped petals on each side until the poppy is as wide as you wish. Use a toothpick or bamboo skewer to needle sculpt the edges of the petals. Make the petals different lengths so that the top edge of the poppy is uneven, like a real flower.

5. Repeat steps 1–4 to make the small poppy unit.

6. Trace the back shapes of the large and small poppies (page 93) onto freezer paper, adding a generous amount to the lower edges to allow for underlap. Cut the templates out.

7. Position the stitched poppy units and the templates for the backs of the poppies on your background fabric. When you are satisfied with the position of these pieces, remove the poppy units. Then press the back templates in position on the background fabric and mark around them.

8. Remove the freezer paper, cut a ³⁄₁₆" allowance inside the marked shapes, and reverse appliqué the poppy backs to the background fabric (see "Technique Tip" on page 90). If you are using three-dimensional stamens, fold them in half and whipstitch them to the poppy backs as shown so that the bottoms of the stamens will lie underneath the front of each poppy when stitched.

9. Appliqué the stitched poppy units on top of the back shapes, referring to the photo on page 88.

TECHNIQUE TIPS

If you like to embroider, consider using pearl cotton or another decorative thread to do long stitches and French knots for the stamens in the poppies. You could also stitch clusters of seed beads at the tops of the long stitches. Investigate other stitch possibilities for hand or machine embroidery as well.

You can be creative in your fabric choices for the reverse-appliquéd under-leaf and the poppy backs. Check out the potential for specialty fabrics with a slight nap, such as corduroy or velveteen, and think about shiny fabrics, like taffeta, satin, or moiré, for the backs of your flowers.

Center shape

Center shape

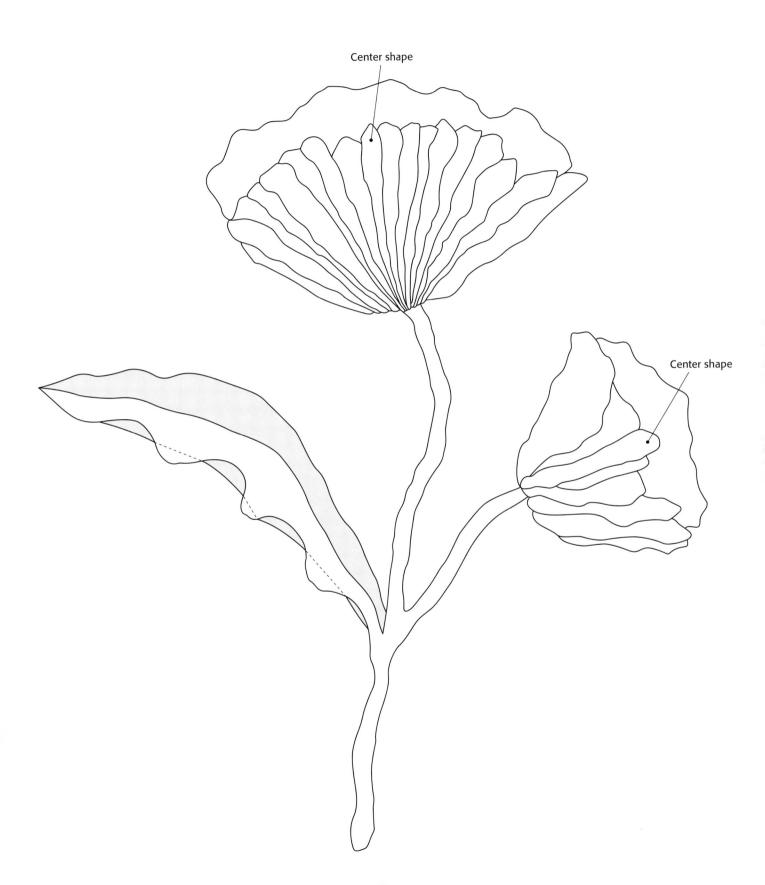

BLEEDING HEARTS

Two fabrics in similar values create a look of three-dimensionality in these faceted stars. Mitered vines with heart-shaped curves echo the curves in the tiny bleeding hearts, and a sprinkling of small leaves adds a delicate touch.

TECHNIQUES

Steep points featuring 2 fabrics (stars)
Unit appliqué (bleeding hearts)
Mitered Hera bias strips (vines)
Inking (stamens)

FABRICS AND SUPPLIES

- One 2" x 42" strip each of 2 different fabrics for large star
- One 1" x 42" strip each of 2 different fabrics for small star, plus scraps of same 2 fabrics for bleeding hearts
- 11" square of fabric for background, plus a 4" square of same fabric for background of small star
- 1 fat quarter each of 2 different fabrics for vines
- Assorted scraps of fabric for leaves
- Sewing machine
- Hera marker
- Black (or other color) Pigma .01 mm marking pen for inking stamens

STITCHING THE LARGE STAR

1. Sew the two 2" x 42" strips for the large star together on a sewing machine, using a ¼" seam allowance. Press the seam allowance toward the fabric you want to appear on the left side of the star points.

2. Trace the large star-point shape (page 101) onto template plastic and cut it out. Place the template on the pressed strip so that both points are exactly aligned with the seam. Mark around the template. Mark a total of 4

star points, allowing at least 1" between the shapes.

3. Cut out each star point with a ¼" seam allowance. Finger-press the right edge of each point shape along the marked turning line and baste it securely in place with a water-soluble glue pen. On the left edge, clip the seam allowance to the marked turning line ¾" down from the point. Below this clip, finger-press the seam allowance and baste it with a water-soluble pen. Make 4 large star points.

4. Finger-press the seam allowance on the bottom-left edge of a star point. Appliqué this folded edge to the bottom-left edge of another star point, matching the marked seam lines. Repeat to make a second half-star unit. Finger-press these seam allowances open.

5. Turn under and finger-press the seam allowance on one half-star unit. Appliqué this folded edge to the other half-star unit, matching the centers. Press the completed large star unit so that each seam is open.

ADDING THE SMALL STAR

1. Sew the 1" x 42" strips for the small star together on a sewing machine, using a ⅛" seam allowance. Press the seam allowance toward the fabric you want to appear on the left side of the star points.

2. Trace the small star-point shape (page 101) onto template plastic and cut it out. Place the template on the pressed strip so that both points are exactly aligned with the seam. Mark around the template. Mark a total of 4 star points, allowing at least 1" between the shapes.

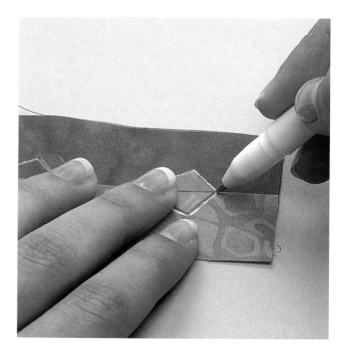

3. Cut out each small star point with a ¼" seam allowance. Finger-press the right edge of each point shape along the marked turning line and baste it securely in place with a water-soluble glue pen. Leave the left edge unglued.

4. Turn under and finger-press the seam allowance on the bottom-left edge of a small star point. Appliqué this folded edge to the bottom-left edge of another small star point. Repeat to make another half-star unit.

5. Turn under and finger-press the seam allowance on one small half-star unit, and appliqué this folded edge to the other small half-star unit.

6. Referring to "Steep Points" on page 15, appliqué the right edge of each small star point to the 4" square of background fabric.

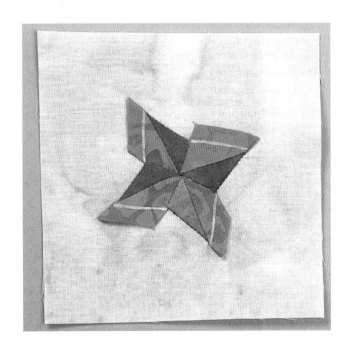

7. Referring to "Steep Points" on page 15, appliqué the left edges of the small star points. Using a circle stencil, mark a circle around the stitched small star.

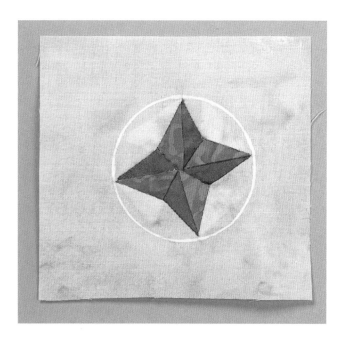

8. Cut a ³⁄₁₆" seam allowance around the marked circle and appliqué it to the center of the large star.

TECHNIQUE TIP

You can eliminate some of the bulk at the center of this block by trimming the excess large star fabric on the wrong side of your work to ¼" inside the appliquéd small star circle.

9. Referring to the photo on page 94 and to "Steep Points" on page 15, appliqué the large star to the background fabric.

ADDING THE VINES

1. Trace the marking guide for the vine stitching lines (page 101) onto template plastic, including the center line, and cut it out. Place the marking guide template over each large star point so that it is 1" from the center point, and mark the stitching line for each vine.

2. Referring to "Hera Bias Strips" on page 14, prepare four ⅛" x 6" Hera bias strips from each of 2 different fabrics for vines.

3. Appliqué a bias strip to a marked curved line, beginning near the right side of the large star point and stitching down to the point of the marked line. Fold the bias strip underneath itself to prepare the turning line for the mitered seam. Insert the second-color bias strip underneath the first-color stitched strip and sew the mitered seam. Trim the fabric underneath the mitered seam to a ³⁄₁₆" seam allowance.

4. Referring to the photo on page 94, sew the remaining portion of the second bias strip to the marked line, ending near the left side of the large star point. Stitch the remaining edges of both bias strips.

5. Repeat steps 3 and 4 to add remaining vines.

ADDING THE BLEEDING HEARTS

1. Trace the left half of the bleeding heart (page 101) onto template plastic, including the dashed line, and cut it out. Mark around this template 8 times on one of the bleeding heart fabrics, including a hatch mark at the beginning and end of the dashed line.

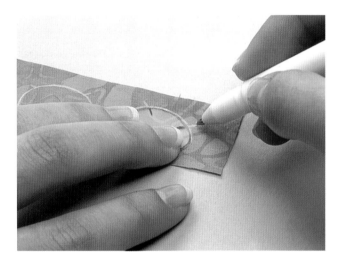

2. Cut a ³⁄₁₆" seam allowance around the bleeding heart shapes and clip at each hatch mark to the marked turning line. Appliqué these shapes to a piece of fabric for the other half of the bleeding hearts, beginning and ending at the hatch marks.

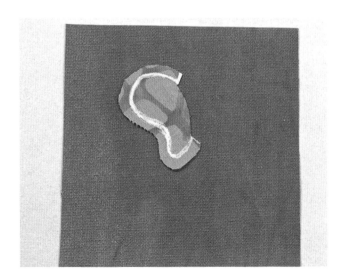

3. Reverse the bleeding heart template and align the dashed line with your stitched line. Mark the second half of each bleeding heart.

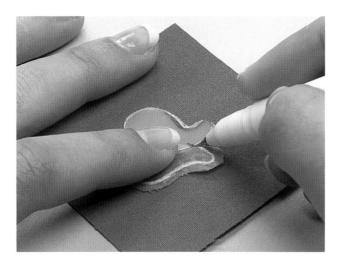

4. Cut a 3/16" seam allowance around the second half of each bleeding heart. Appliqué a bleeding heart at the end of each vine, referring to the photo on page 94.

5. Using a black Pigma .01 mm marking pen, add 3 to 5 small lines for stamens at the center of each bleeding heart, referring to the photo on page 94. Make these lines delicately and randomly, thickening the tips slightly.

ADDING THE LEAVES

1. Trace the leaf shape (page 101) onto template plastic and cut it out. Mark a total of 72 leaf shapes on assorted leaf fabrics.

2. Cut a 3/16" seam allowance around each leaf shape. Appliqué 18 leaves on each vine, referring to the photo on page 94 for placement. Let these leaves be slightly different in shape, and don't worry about the angles of the leaves on each vine. The repetition of so many leaves makes it impossible for the eye to perceive slight irregularities in position or shape.

◆◆◆

COLOR-BLENDING TIP

Mix light, medium, and dark values of leaves randomly so you can position the colors to show up well against both your background fabric and your large star fabric.

◆◆◆

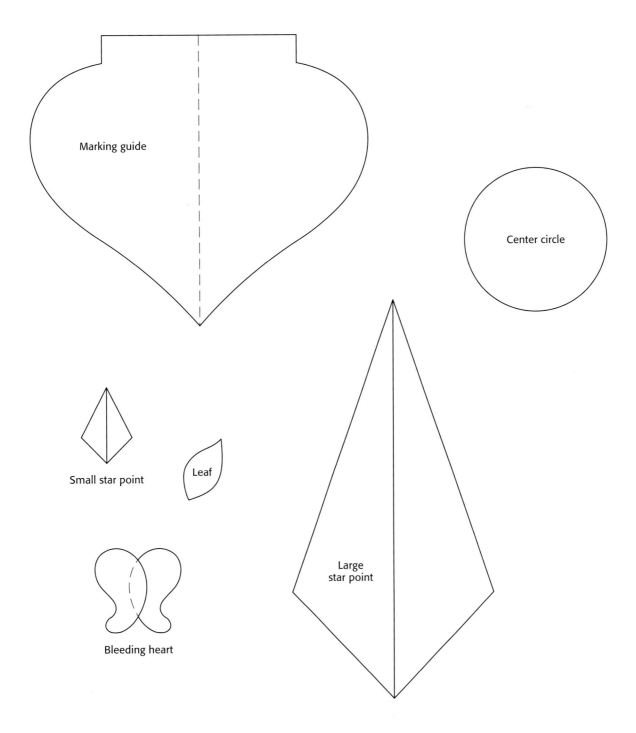

Marking guide

Center circle

Small star point

Leaf

Large
star point

Bleeding heart

BIRDS-OF-PARADISE

Flame-bright tips and curvy, paddle-shaped leaves make the bird-of-paradise unlike any other flower. Choose fiery oranges, reds, golds, yellows—even red-purples for the tips, and use my steep-point technique to stitch them with ease.

TECHNIQUES

Color blending (leaves)

Unit appliqué (birds-of-paradise, leaves)

Steep points (birds-of-paradise)

Sandwiching very thin strips of contrast color between narrow
     shapes (leaves)

FABRICS AND SUPPLIES

COLOR-BLENDING TIP

Color blending several fabrics in graduated
values for the leaf tops creates the effect of
light shining on the surface of the leaves.
Think of other large leaf shapes where you
might use this technique to advantage.

- 16 assorted 3" squares of fabric for leaf tops
- ⅛ yd. of fabric for leaf veins
- 1 fat quarter of fabric for leaf bottoms
- 1 fat quarter of fabric for main portion of flowers
- 16 assorted 3" squares of fabric for top edges and points of flowers
- Two 4" squares of fabric for lower portions of flowers
- 11" square of fabric for background

STITCHING THE LEAF TOPS

1. Trace the right leaf and left leaf shapes (page 107) onto freezer paper, including the hatch marks, and add ½" to the ends of the stems to allow for underlap. Cut out the leaf shapes. Number the shapes in the top section of each leaf from 1 to 8 as shown.

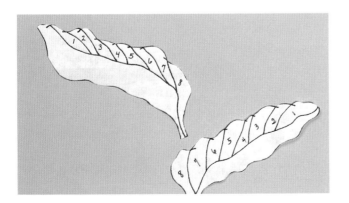

2. Cut the top section from the left leaf template. Cut out shape 1 and press it onto a 3" square of fabric. Mark around the shape, including the hatch mark.

3. Remove the freezer paper and cut a ½" seam allowance all the way around shape 1. Wider seam allowances make unit appliqué easier. On the edge where shape 1 will join shape 2, trim the seam allowance to ³⁄₁₆".

4. Stitch shape 1 to a 3" square of fabric for shape 2, ending at the hatch mark. Cut shape 2 from the template and press it next to your stitched line. Mark around shape 2. Cut a ½" seam allowance around shape 2.

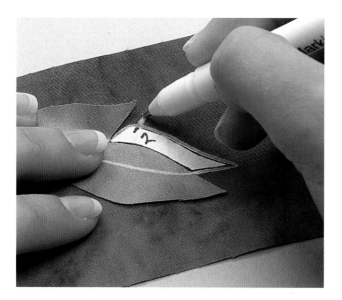

5. Repeat steps 2–4 to add shapes 3–8, completing the top section of the left leaf.

6. Repeat steps 2–5 for the top section of the right leaf.

ADDING THE VEINS AND LOWER LEAVES

1. Cut out and stitch the lower section of the left leaf to a piece of fabric for the leaf vein. Trim the vein fabric to a scant ¼" from your stitched line.

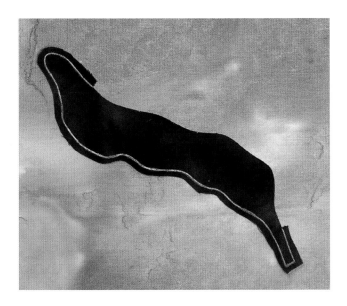

2. Clip the vein fabric to ⅛" from the stitched line wherever there are inner curves, and finger-press the vein fabric to less than ⅛" wide. Stitch the folded vein fabric to the top leaf section.

3. Repeat steps 1 and 2 for the right leaf.

STITCHING THE BIRD-OF-PARADISE FLOWERS

1. Trace the bird-of-paradise shapes (page 107) onto freezer paper, including the hatch marks, and cut them out. Press the templates onto the main flower fabric and mark around them, including the hatch marks.

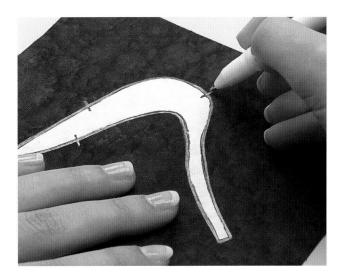

2. Remove the freezer paper. Stitch the top edge of the left-facing flower to a 3" square of fabric, beginning and ending at the hatch marks.

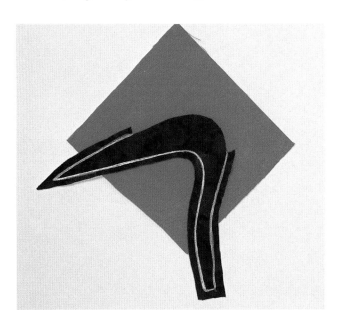

3. Trim this fabric to a scant ¼" from your stitched line, allowing ¼" extra at each end of the seam.

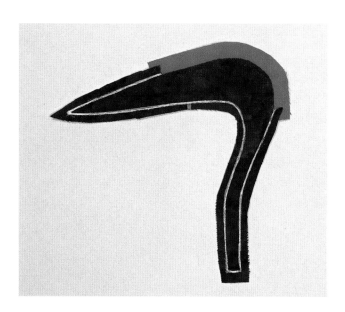

4. Stitch the lower edge of the flower unit to a 4" square of fabric, beginning and ending at the hatch marks. Trim this fabric to ¼" from your stitched line, allowing ¼" extra at each end.

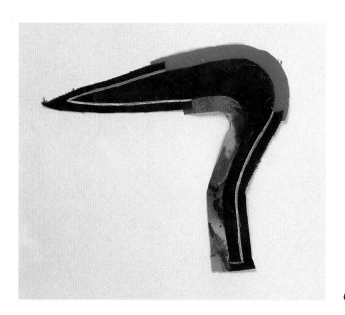

5. Repeat steps 2–4 to stitch the right-facing bird-of-paradise flower.

PUTTING IT ALL TOGETHER

1. Arrange the bird-of-paradise flowers and the leaves on the background fabric, referring to the photo on page 102. Fold and finger-press the upper edge on the flowers to a narrow width. Do the same for the lower areas of the flowers, folding them to a ⅛" width and clipping inner curves where necessary. Stitch the flower units on the background fabric, referring to "Steep Points" on page 15. Stitch the leaves in place, overlapping the stems.

2. Trace the point shapes for the top of each flower (page 107) onto freezer paper and cut them out. Press the point templates onto squares of fabric and mark around them. Cut the points out with a ³⁄₁₆" seam allowance on the right edge and a ¼" seam allowance on the left edge. Stitch the points at the top of each bird-of-paradise flower, referring to the photo on page 102 and to "Steep Points" on page 15.

Note: ✕ indicates placement
of narrow band of color.

TULIPS

Sunlight glinting on a real tulip gave me the idea of using sheer metallic fabric for hand appliqué. In this design, I covered one petal in the large tulip and part of the bud with a shimmery blue metallic sheer, and I let the folds peek out along the edges to create a hint of transparency. I stippled the edges of the finished petals with orange, pink, blue, and brown marking pens to give the fabrics a satinlike sheen.

TECHNIQUES

Color blending (stems)

Unit appliqué (tulip, bud)

Steep points featuring 2 or 3 fabrics (leaves)

Using metallic sheers (large tulip petal)

Inking (tulip, bud)

Sandwiching very thin strips of contrast color between narrow
    shapes (leaves)

FABRICS AND SUPPLIES

- 2 fat quarters of fabric for leaves and stem
- 1 fat quarter of fabric for leaf veins and stem
- Assorted 4" squares of fabric for tulip and bud
- 6" square of sheer metallic fabric for tulip and bud
- 11" square of fabric for background
- Orange, pink, brown, and blue Pigma .01 mm marking pens for inking tulip and bud

STITCHING THE STEM

1. Trace the stem shape (page 114) onto freezer paper and cut it out. Press the stem template onto a piece of fabric and mark around it. Remove the freezer paper and cut the stem out on the marked lines (no seam allowances).

2. Stitch the right edges of the stem to another piece of fabric.

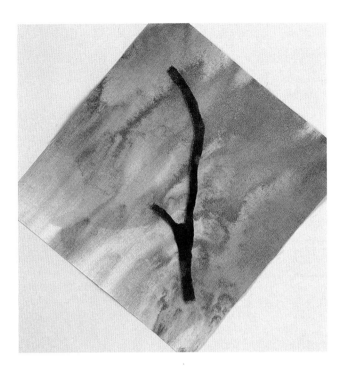

3. Trim this fabric to a scant ¼" from the stitched lines.

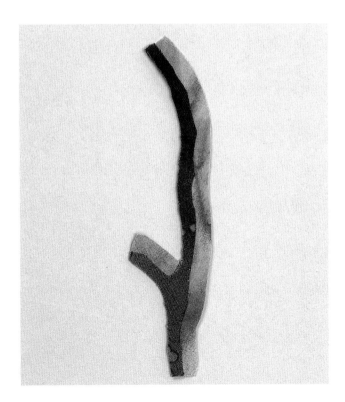

STITCHING THE LEAVES

1. Trace the leaf shapes (page 114) onto freezer paper and cut them out. Cut each template apart on the center line. Press the inner portion of one leaf template onto a piece of fabric and mark around it. Remove the freezer paper and cut a ³⁄₁₆" seam allowance around the inner-leaf shape.

COLOR-BLENDING TIP

When you add very narrow strips of color between 2 appliqué shapes, such as the center veins in these leaves, try using multicolored fabrics rather than tone-on-tone prints or solids. The variations in color will make the center vein shimmer with light along the entire leaf.

2. Stitch the top curve of the inner-leaf shape to a piece of fabric for leaf veins.

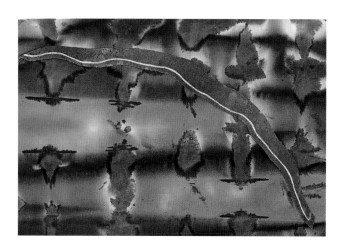

3. Trim the vein fabric to a scant ¼" from the stitched line and clip to ⅛" from the stitched line, spacing these clips approximately ¼" apart. Trim the excess vein fabric underneath the leaf shape.

4. Fold the vein fabric to a very narrow width and finger-press the fold. Stitch the folded vein to a piece of fabric for the outer leaf.

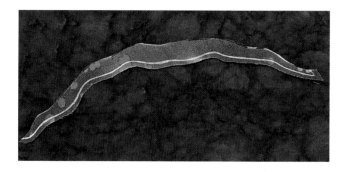

5. Press the outer-leaf template next to your stitched line at the center of the leaf (covering the vein), and mark around it. Cut a 3/16" seam allowance around the outer-leaf shape.

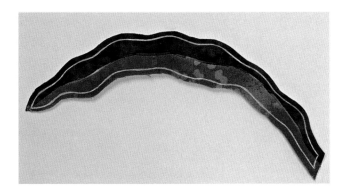

6. Repeat steps 1–5 to make the second leaf unit.

STITCHING THE TULIP

1. Trace the tulip shape (page 114) onto freezer paper and cut it out. Cut the right-center petal from the tulip shape and press it onto a square of fabric. Mark around the template, remove the freezer paper, and cut a 3/16" seam allowance around this shape. Repeat for the left-center petal.

2. Stitch the right-center petal to a square of fabric for the center area.

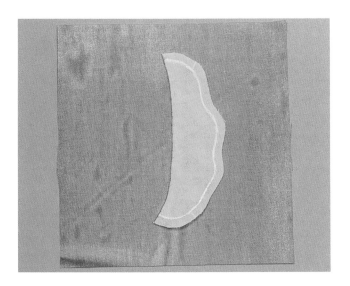

TECHNIQUE TIP

Before you use a sheer metallic fabric for appliqué, test it by pressing it between 2 pieces of cotton fabric with your iron set on the cotton setting. If the sheer fabric curls, melts, distorts, or develops holes, it's not suitable for appliqué. Work only with fabrics that pass the press test.

3. Pin a square of sheer metallic fabric over the left-center petal and roughly cut a 1/4" seam allowance around the petal shape. Turn under the sheer metallic and the cotton fabric along the right edge of the left-center petal, and appliqué it to the square of center fabric, approximately 1/8" from the right-center petal.

4. Trim the center fabric to 3/16" from the top and bottom of the center area. Also trim it to a 3/16" seam allowance on the back side of your work. Stitch the left edge of the left-center petal to a piece of fabric for the next side petal, allowing a bit of the sheer fabric to extend beyond your stitching line. Cut the

111

next petal shape from the tulip template and press it next to your stitched line, taking care not to let the iron come directly in contact with the sheer metallic fabric. Mark around this shape, remove the freezer paper, and cut a ³⁄₁₆" seam allowance around it.

5. Repeat step 4 to add the remaining petals on the left side of the tulip, as well as the remaining petals on the right side of the tulip. Stitch the top edge of the tulip unit to a piece of fabric for the tulip back. Cut out and press the template for the tulip back next to your stitched line. Mark around it, remove the freezer paper, and cut a ³⁄₁₆" seam allowance around the tulip back.

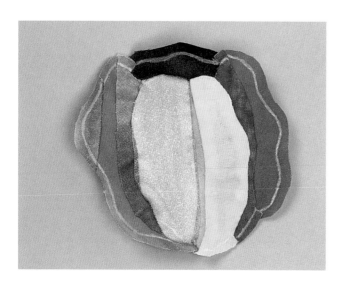

STITCHING THE BUD

1. Trace the bud shape (page 114) onto freezer paper, including the hatch marks, and cut it out. Cut out the center shape and press it onto a square of fabric. Mark around it and remove the freezer paper. Cut a ³⁄₁₆" seam allowance around the shape and clip to the hatch marks.

2. Stitch the left edge of the bud center to a square of fabric covered with sheer metallic fabric, starting and ending at the hatch marks. Place (don't press) the left side template next to your stitching line on the left side of the bud and mark around it. Stitch the right edge of the bud center to a square of fabric for the right petal. Press the right side template next to your stitching line on the right edge of the bud and mark around it; remove the freezer paper. On the metallic fabric, cut a ¼" seam allowance around the left side shape. Cut a ³⁄₁₆" seam allowance around both of the *cotton* fabric side bud shapes. Trim the excess fabric underneath to ³⁄₁₆" from your stitched lines.

PUTTING IT ALL TOGETHER

1. Referring to the photo on page 108, stitch the stem on the background fabric, followed by the large tulip unit and the bud unit.

2. Stitch the leaves on the background fabric, referring to "Steep Points" on page 15.

3. Referring to the photo on page 108 for guidance, use Pigma .01 mm marking pens in various colors to stipple tiny dots along the sides of the tulip petals and bud shapes. You can stipple through sheer metallic fabric just as easily as on cotton. Hold your pen vertically as you add tiny dots, and work quickly so that the ink will not bleed into the fabric and create larger areas of color than you may want.

TECHNIQUE TIP

Make several black-and-white photocopies of your finished block and use them to practice various stippling effects on your tulip and bud. When you have created the look you like, you'll be confident taking a pigma pen to fabric.

113

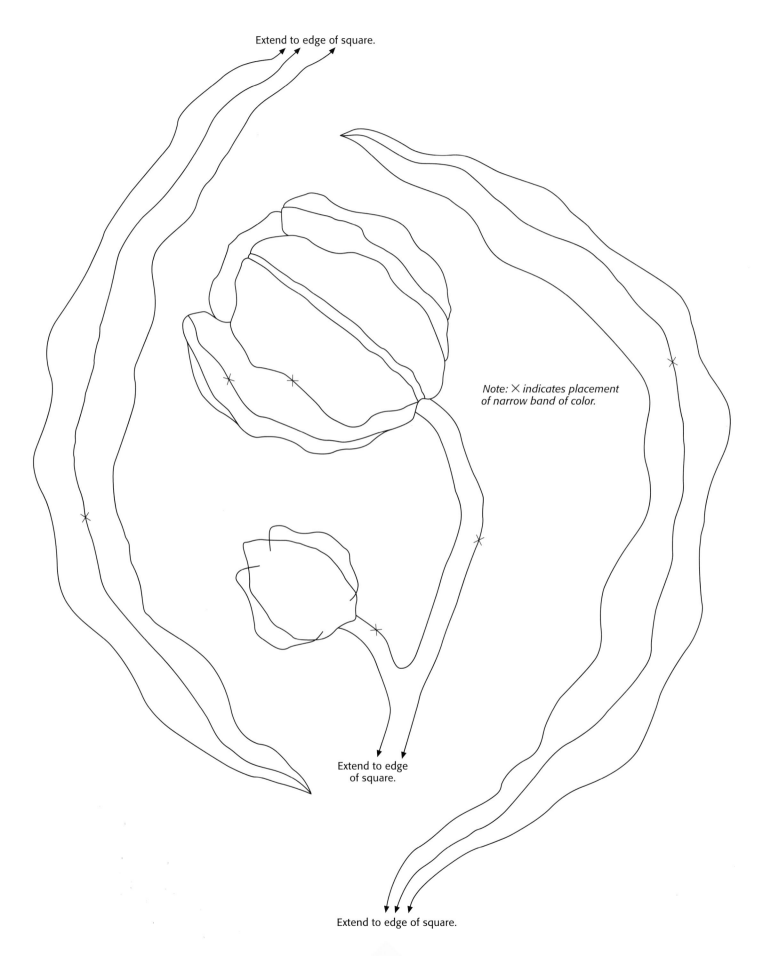

Extend to edge of square.

Note: ✕ indicates placement
of narrow band of color.

Extend to edge
of square.

Extend to edge of square.

ROSE

I do not know of any other flower that comes in as many beautiful colors as a rose. In this design, I wanted to create the effect of sunshine and shadow bringing out many colors within a single flower. Color blend a wide variety of dark, medium, and light fabrics in your favorite colors, and include an accent or two from another color family, such as the yellow and dark purple in my rose.

TECHNIQUES

Color blending (rose)

Unit appliqué (rose)

Hera bias strips (stems)

Tiny random points (serrated leaves)

Inking (leaf veins)

FABRICS AND SUPPLIES

- 1 fat quarter each of 2 different contrast fabrics for stems
- 11" square of fabric for background
- Wide assortment of dark, medium, and light scrap fabrics in various colors for rose
- Sixteen 3" squares for leaves
- 1 fat quarter of fabric for serrated portions of leaves
- Hera marker
- Black Pigma .01 mm marking pen for inking leaves

STITCHING THE STEMS

1. Referring to "Hera-Bias Strips" on page 14, make three ¼" x 10" stems. Stitch one side of each stem to a piece of fabric for the other half of each stem, placing the stems on the bias.

2. Trim the fabric to ¼" from your stitched lines. Also trim the excess fabric underneath the stems. Turn under and finger-press these edges of the stems, shaping them so that they are slightly wider toward the bottom and narrower toward the top of each stem.

3. Trace the stem stitching lines from page 121 onto your background fabric and stitch the shaped stems in place.

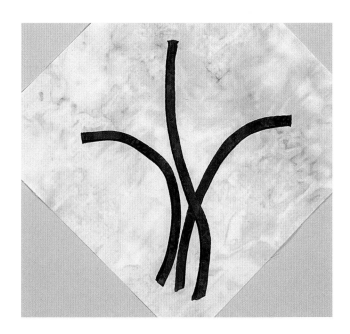

STITCHING THE ROSE

1. Trace the rose shape from page 122 onto freezer paper, including the hatch marks and numbers, and cut it out.

2. Cut shape 1 from the template, and press it onto a piece of fabric. Mark around the template and remove the freezer paper. Cut shape 1 out with a ½" seam allowance.

3. Stitch the right edge of shape 1 to a piece of fabric for shape 2. Cut shape 2 from the rose template and press it next to the stitched line. Mark around shape 2 and remove the freezer paper. Cut a ½" seam allowance around the bottom of shape 2.

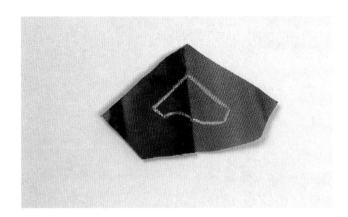

4. Stitch the right edge of shape 2 to a piece of fabric for shape 3. Cut shape 3 from the rose template and press it next to your stitched line on shape 2. Mark around shape 3 and remove the freezer paper. Cut a ½" seam allowance around the bottom of shape 3 and a ³⁄₁₆" seam allowance around the remaining edges.

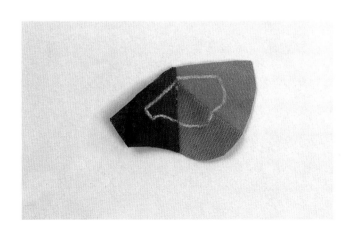

5. Stitch the top edge of shapes 1, 2, and 3 to a piece of fabric for shape 4. Cut out and press the template for shape 4 next to your stitching line and mark around it. Remove the freezer paper, and cut a ½" seam allowance around shape 4.

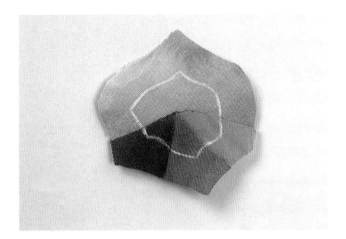

6. In the same manner, stitch shapes 5–8 together, leaving a ½" seam allowance at the bottom edge of the unit for underlap.

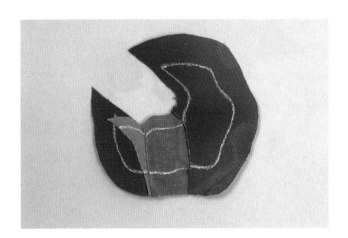

7. Stitch shapes 9–11 together, cutting a ³⁄₁₆"
   seam allowance around the entire unit except
   at the bottom edge as shown.

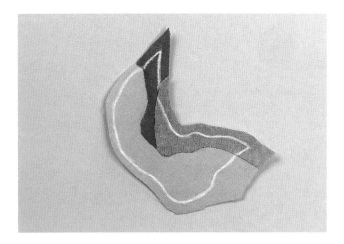

8. Stitch shapes 12 and 13 together, cutting a
   ³⁄₁₆" seam allowance around the unit.

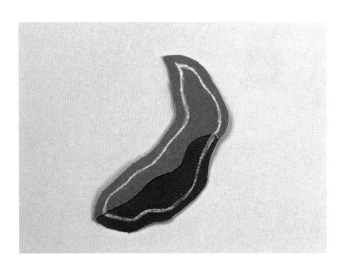

9. Sew shapes 14–20 together, adding a *generous*
   ½" seam allowance to the bottom edge of
   each shape so that there will be extra fabric
   for underlap inside the joined unit.

10. Stitch the units from steps 5–8 together.
    Then stitch the joined units to the center of
    the unit from step 9. Press the completed rose
    unit.

STITCHING THE SERRATED LEAVES

1. Trace a leaf pattern from page 122 onto template plastic and cut it out. Mark around the leaf template 16 times on assorted fabrics. Cut a ³⁄₁₆" seam allowance around each leaf shape.

COLOR-BLENDING TIP

Let the leaves in your block echo some of the colors in your rose. Just a hint of purple, red, pink, gold, or blue adds visual interest to green leaves. Sprinkle these accent hues evenly throughout the leaves in your block so that the effect is balanced. You might also do as I did and make the leaves on one side of your rose a tiny bit lighter than the leaves on the other side.

2. Stitch each leaf to the fabric for the serrated edges. Mark random point shapes (serrations) around each leaf. These lines will be used *only* as guidelines when stitching the serrations.

TECHNIQUE TIP

Use a closely woven fabric such as a batik for the underlayer of the leaves in this block to avoid fraying when you stitch the serrated edges.

3. Practice stitching a serrated leaf on a scrap piece of background fabric before you start stitching the leaves onto the stems on your actual background square. This will give you confidence in stitching the tiny points. Start by cutting a ⅛" seam allowance around the angled lines.

4. Starting near the bottom point of the leaf, begin stitching the serrations, letting your drawn line be just a guideline. I like to turn my drawn lines under enough so that the points extend only a short distance from the stitched top-leaf shape. When you reach the next point, clip the fabric at the angled area all the way up to the stitched leaf. Use a toothpick or bamboo skewer to tuck the fabric under against the stitched leaf shape, allowing only a small point to remain visible.

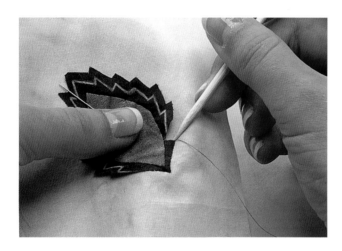

5. When you like the look of the first serration, stitch it in place, and end by bringing your needle up at the very edge of the stitched top-leaf shape. Continue stitching the remaining serrations in the same manner.

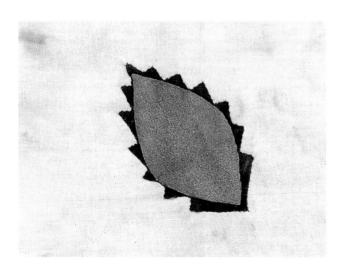

PUTTING IT ALL TOGETHER

1. Arrange the 16 prepared leaves and the rose unit on the stitched stems on your background fabric, referring to the photo on page 115.

2. Remove the rose unit and stitch the serrated leaves in place, followed by the rose unit.

3. Using a black .01 mm Pigma marking pen, add random veins to each leaf. Start by drawing from one point of a leaf to the opposite point to create a center vein. Add feathery, delicate side veins with random curves and angles on each side of the center vein.

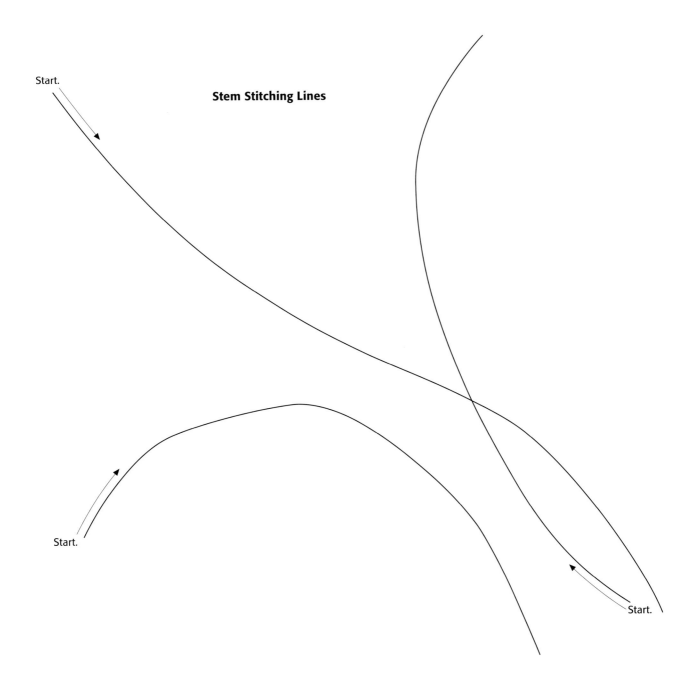

Stem Stitching Lines

Start.

Start.

Start.

RESOURCES

To FIND products mentioned in this book, contact the following companies.

ANDOVER FABRICS
1359 Broadway
New York, NY 10018
800-223-5678
www.andoverfabrics.com

Fabrics designed by Jane Townswick

THE FLYING QUILTER
732-925-4870
the flyingquilter@yahoo.com

Customized long-arm machine quilting. Price list available from Terry P. Clark.

GAIL KESSLER
Ladyfingers Sewing Studio
6375 Oley Turnpike Road
Oley, PA 19547
610-689-0068
Fax: 610-689-0067
www.ladyfingerssewing.com
Hours: Thursday 10–8; Friday and Saturday
10–5 (closed Sunday through Wednesday)

General sewing supplies, quilt fabrics, block-of-the month kits, 3½" serrated embroidery scissors, CAT paper, YLI silk thread in size 100 (all colors), Kinkamé silk thread in size 50 (all colors)

JEANA KIMBALL'S FOXGLOVE COTTAGE
PO Box 698
Santa Clara, UT 84765
foxglovecottage@ifox.com

Size #11 straw needles

MICKEY LAWLER'S SKYDYES
PO Box 370116
West Hartford, CT 06137-0116
860-232-1429
Fax: 860-236-9117
Skydyes@aol.com
www.skydyes.com

Hand-painted cottons and silks, fabric paints

YLI CORPORATION
161 West Main Street
Rock Hill, SC 29730
800-296-8139 or 803-985-3100
Fax: 803-985-3106
www.ylicorp.com

100%-silk threads (catalog $1)

ABOUT THE AUTHOR

JANE TOWNSWICK is an accomplished author, editor, quilter, teacher, and former quilt-shop owner who has developed amazing expertise in hand appliqué. She has been a guest artist and instructor at Elly Sienkiewicz's esteemed Appliqué Academy, and her work has been featured in *Quilter's Newsletter Magazine* and *American Quilter* magazine. She is the author of *Artful Appliqué: The Easy Way* (2000) and *Artful Album Quilts: Appliqué Inspirations from Traditional Blocks* (2001), both published by Martingale & Company. Jane quilts and teaches appliqué in her hometown of Allentown, Pennsylvania, as well as throughout the country.

new and bestselling titles from

America's Best-Loved Craft & Hobby Books™

America's Best-Loved Quilt Books®

NEW RELEASES
1000 Great Quilt Blocks
American Stenciled Quilts
Americana Quilts
Appliquilt in the Cabin
Bed and Breakfast Quilts
Best of Black Mountain Quilts, The
Beyond the Blocks
Blissful Bath, The
Celebrations!
Color-Blend Appliqué
Fabulous Quilts from Favorite Patterns
Feathers That Fly
Handcrafted Garden Accents
Handprint Quilts
Knitted Throws and More for the Simply
    Beautiful Home
Knitter's Book of Finishing Techniques, The
Knitter's Template, A
Make Room for Christmas Quilts
More Paintbox Knits
Painted Whimsies
Patriotic Little Quilts
Quick Quilts Using Quick Bias
Quick-Change Quilts
Quilts for Mantels and More
Snuggle Up
Split-Diamond Dazzlers
Stack the Deck!
Strips and Strings
Sweet Dreams
Treasury of Rowan Knits, A
Triangle Tricks
Triangle-Free Quilts

APPLIQUÉ
Artful Album Quilts
Artful Appliqué
Blossoms in Winter
Easy Art of Appliqué, The
Fun with Sunbonnet Sue
Sunbonnet Sue All through the Year

BABY QUILTS
Easy Paper-Pieced Baby Quilts
Even More Quilts for Baby
More Quilts for Baby
Play Quilts
Quilted Nursery, The
Quilts for Baby

HOLIDAY QUILTS
Christmas at That Patchwork Place®
Christmas Cats and Dogs
Creepy Crafty Halloween
Handcrafted Christmas, A
Welcome to the North Pole

LEARNING TO QUILT
Joy of Quilting, The
Nickel Quilts
Quick Watercolor Quilts
Quilts from Aunt Amy
Simple Joys of Quilting, The
Your First Quilt Book (or it should be!)

PAPER PIECING
40 Bright and Bold Paper-Pieced Blocks
50 Fabulous Paper-Pieced Stars
For the Birds
Quilter's Ark, A
Rich Traditions

ROTARY CUTTING
101 Fabulous Rotary-Cut Quilts
365 Quilt Blocks a Year Perpetual Calendar
Around the Block Again
Around the Block with Judy Hopkins
Log Cabin Fever
More Fat Quarter Quilts

TOPICS IN QUILTMAKING
Batik Beauties
Frayed-Edge Fun
Log Cabin Fever
Machine Quilting Made Easy
Quick Watercolor Quilts
Reversible Quilts

CRAFTS
300 Papermaking Recipes
ABCs of Making Teddy Bears, The
Creating with Paint
Handcrafted Frames
Painted Chairs
Stamp in Color
Stamp with Style

KNITTING & CROCHET
365 Knitting Stitches a Year Perpetual
    Calendar
Clever Knits
Crochet for Babies and Toddlers
Crocheted Sweaters
Irresistible Knits
Knitted Shawls, Stoles, and Scarves
Knitted Sweaters for Every Season
Knitting with Novelty Yarns
Paintbox Knits
Simply Beautiful Sweaters
Simply Beautiful Sweaters for Men
Too Cute! Cotton Knits for Toddlers
Ultimate Knitter's Guide, The

Our books are available at bookstores and your favorite craft, fabric, and yarn
retailers. If you don't see the title you're looking for, visit us at
www.martingale-pub.com or contact us at:

1-800-426-3126

International: 1-425-483-3313

Fax: 1-425-486-7596

E-mail: info@martingale-pub.com

For more information and a full list of our titles, visit our Web site.